江汉大学研究生教材建设项目成果
江汉大学外国语学院教材资助项目成果

英美散文批评教程

刘晓燕　舒玲娥　李欣怡　主编

华中科技大学出版社
http://press.hust.edu.cn
中国·武汉

内容提要

本书共 16 章,介绍了关于 16 位英美著名散文家的批评文章,跨越了整个英美文学史的多个历史时期。这些批评文章从不同的批评视角,运用不同的批评理论,采用不同的批评方法,对 16 位散文家及其作品的背景、文本、结构和主题等进行分析,具有一定的代表性。书后附录部分精选了每位散文家各 1 篇散文,供读者结合教材内容进行鉴赏。本教材可供本科生和研究生教学使用,教学重点在于让学生掌握散文批评文章的写作思路和批评方法。

图书在版编目(CIP)数据

英美散文批评教程 / 刘晓燕, 舒玲娥, 李欣怡主编. -- 武汉:华中科技大学出版社, 2024.8. -- (普通高等学校"十四五"规划英语数字化精品教材). -- ISBN 978-7-5772-1098-8

Ⅰ. H319.4

中国国家版本馆 CIP 数据核字第 2024Q48W74 号

英美散文批评教程　　　　　　　　　　刘晓燕　舒玲娥　李欣怡　主编
Yingmei Sanwen Piping Jiaocheng

策划编辑:	刘　平
责任编辑:	江旭玉
封面设计:	原色设计
责任校对:	张汇娟
责任监印:	周治超
出版发行:	华中科技大学出版社(中国·武汉)　电话:(027)81321913
	武汉市东湖新技术开发区华工科技园　邮编:430223
录　　排:	华中科技大学出版社美编室
印　　刷:	武汉开心印刷有限公司
开　　本:	787mm×1092mm　1/16
印　　张:	10
字　　数:	297 千字
版　　次:	2024 年 8 月第 1 版第 1 次印刷
定　　价:	48.00 元

本书若有印装质量问题,请向出版社营销中心调换
全国免费服务热线:400-6679-118　竭诚为您服务
版权所有　侵权必究

Contents

Chapter 1   Francis Bacon   /1

Chapter 2   Jonathan Swift   /11

Chapter 3   Joseph Addison   /16

Chapter 4   Samuel Johnson   /20

Chapter 5   Charles Lamb   /26

Chapter 6   William Hazlitt   /30

Chapter 7   Thomas De Quincey   /35

Chapter 8   Bertrand Russell   /44

Chapter 9   Virginia Woolf   /46

Chapter 10   George Orwell   /51

Chapter 11   John Boynton Priestley   /56

Chapter 12   Benjamin Franklin   /59

Chapter 13   Ralph Waldo Emerson   /65

Chapter 14   Henry David Thoreau   /83

Chapter 15   Mark Twain   /103

Chapter 16   Elwyn Brooks White   /106

Appendix   /109

Chapter 1
Francis Bacon

Francis Bacon (1561-1626)

Francis Bacon was one of the leading figures in natural philosophy and in the field of scientific methodology in the period of transition from the Renaissance to the early modern era. As a lawyer, statesman, philosopher, and master of the English tongue, he is remembered in literary terms for the sharp worldly wisdom of a few dozen essays; by students of constitutional history for his power as a speaker in Parliament and in famous trials and as James Ⅰ's lord chancellor; and intellectually as a man who claimed all knowledge as his province and, after a magisterial survey, urgently advocated new ways by which man might establish a legitimate command over nature for the relief of his estate.[①]

---

① https://www.britannica.com/biography/Francis-Bacon-Viscount-Saint-Alban.

Critical Perspectives

1. Philosophical Study

J. Marianne Siegmund, in "Knowledge: Domination or Genuine Service?", argues that "Francis Bacon is known for equating knowledge and power. Today, one might interpret his idea of knowledge as an electronic club to manipulate others". In this essay, the author examines one's relation to knowledge in terms of a receptivity that might be described as service. Whether one actually treats another in harmony with relation to knowledge remains, of course, a matter of one's free will. Nevertheless, at the level of being, the person is more fittingly described as a humble servant of the truth and of one another rather than as a domineering figure seeking to manipulate.[①]

Caryn O'Connell, in "Bacon's Hints: The *Sylva Sylvarum*'s Intimate Science", refers that "Through an analysis of Bacon's last natural history, this essay sketches a less familiar Baconianism, one that deemphasizes inductive method; that does not lead inevitably toward ideals of objectivity; and that nurtures a mode of doing science that is maculately intimate. It begins by locating the *Sylva* in the context of Aristotle's *Problems* and Giambattista della Porta's *Natural Magick*. Bacon, it shows, takes the experimental ethos and compositional engine of the latter (hands-on, process analysis) and runs them up against the philosophized mundane phenomena of the former (e.g., thirst, perspiration), in order to craft the conditions for readers to recognize their own ontological and epistemological grip on fundamental physical principles. The *Sylva* is not, then, the miscellany it was long considered to be, but a painstakingly ordered training manual. To bear out this claim, the essay surveys some of the text's seventeenth-century imitators. What emerges is a Baconian practice in which practitioners have been taught not to misgive or deny but to trust their lived experiences, which, be they never so private, are always broadly shared and thus philosophically freighted".[②]

Nico Stehr, and Marian T. Adolf, in "Knowledge/Power/Resistance", present that "Francis Bacon's famous metaphor that knowledge is power has been the intellectual springboard for many scholars to offer misleading observations about the inordinate authority and power of

---

① Siegmund J M. "Knowledge: Domination or Genuine Service?". Catholic Social Science Review, 2021(26): 223-233.
② O'Connell C. "Bacon's Hints: The *Sylva Sylvarum*'s Intimate Science". Studies in Philology, 2016, 113(3): 634-667.

knowledge. Among the important implications that Bacon derives from his metaphor is the assertion that individuals provided with experimental skills and practical knowledge are those most entitled to hold executive office, rather than the aristocracy of blood. In this essay, we critically analyze Michel Foucault's ambivalent version of the closeness of knowledge, power and authority".①

Allison Machlis Meyer, in "The Politics of Queenship in Francis Bacon's *The History of the Reign of King Henry Ⅶ* and John Ford's *Perkin Warbeck*", argues that scholarly attention to Francis Bacon's *The History of the Reign of King Henry Ⅶ* has missed the political import of the text's criticisms of Henry VII's relationship with his wife, Elizabeth York, while approaches to John Ford's *Perkin Warbeck* have overlooked the play's intertextual engagement with *The History*'s view of royal marriage. "In this essay, I argue that Bacon identifies a monarch's policies toward his queen consort as central to that monarch's successes or failures through an intentionally fictive account of Henry Ⅶ's oppression and estrangement of Elizabeth, a view of monarchal politics that emerges in response to James Ⅰ's negotiation of relationships with his female kin. As *Perkin Warbeck* answers the questions about royal marriage posed in *The History* by promoting a fantasy of apolitical queenship, it also critiques the political influence of Queen Henrietta Maria in the early years of Charles Ⅰ's reign".②

Rose-Mary Sargent, in "Francis Bacon and the Humanistic Aspects of Modernity", focuses on various works of philosopher Francis Bacon regarding the humanistic aspects of modernity. Topics discussed include the author's views on how Bacon's works have been interpreted by critics and historians; information on Bacon's works *The Advancement of Learning*, *The New Organon*, *The Great Instauration*, which reflect his humanist education; and discussion on Bacon and modernity in his works.③

Peter Pesic, in "Francis Bacon, Violence, and the Motion of Liberty: The Aristotelian Background", discusses English philosopher Francis Bacon's use of the term violence and examines its origins in the philosophies of the Greek philosopher Aristotle. It analyzes Aristotle's technical use of the term violence and how authors and philosophers prior to Bacon referred to the term, Bacon's use of the term in his writings and whether he used the term to support a violence toward nature, and Bacon's understanding of violence leading to his concept of the motion of liberty.④

---

① Stehr N, Adolf M T. "Knowledge/ Power/ Resistance". Society, 2018(55): 193-198.
② Meyer A M. "The Politics of Queenship in Francis Bacon's *The History of the Reign of King Henry Ⅶ* and John Ford's *Perkin Warbeck*". Studies in Philology, 2014, 111(2): 312-345.
③ Sargent R-M. "Francis Bacon and the Humanistic Aspects of Modernity". Midwest Studies in Philosophy, 2002, 26(1): 124-139.
④ Pesic P. "Francis Bacon, Violence, and the Motion of Liberty: The Aristotelian Background". Journal of the History of Ideas, 2014, 75(1): 69-90.

Guido Giglioni, in "Philosophy according to Tacitus: Francis Bacon and the Inquiry into the Limits of Human Self-Delusion", argues that "Bacon belonged to a cultural milieu that, between the sixteenth and the seventeenth centuries, proved to be especially receptive to influences coming from such continental authors as Machiavelli, Bodin, Duplessis-Mornay, Hotman, and, through Lipsius, a particular brand of Stoicism tinged with Tacitean motifs. Within the broader question of Tacitus' influence on Tudor and Stuart culture, this article focuses on the issue of how Bacon's characteristic insistence on the powers of the imagination (fingere) and of belief (credere) in shaping human history may have influenced his view that human beings suffer from an innate tendency to self-delusion".[1]

Jan Schmidt, in "The Renaissance of Francis Bacon", discusses that the program of intervening, manipulating, constructing and creating is central to natural and engineering sciences. "A renewed wave of interest in this program has emerged within the recent practices and discourse of nano-technoscience. However, it is striking that, framed from the perspective of well-established epistemologies, the constructed technoscientific objects and engineered things remain invisible. Their ontological and epistemological status is unclear. The purpose of the present paper is to support present-day approaches to techno-objects ('ontology') insofar as they make these hidden objects epistemologically perceivable. To accomplish this goal, it is inspiring to look back to the origin of the project of modernity and to its founding father: Francis Bacon". The thesis argues that everything we need today for an adequate (dialectic-materialist), ontologically well-informed epistemology of technoscience can be found in the works of Bacon—this position will be called epistemological real-constructivism. "Rather than describing it as realist or constructivist, empiricist or rationalist, Bacon's position can best be understood as real-constructivist since it challenges modern dichotomies, including the dichotomy between epistemology and ontology. Such real-constructive turn might serve to promote the acknowledgement that natural and engineering sciences, in particular recent technosciences, are creating and producing the world we live in. Reflection upon the contemporary relevance of Bacon is intended as a contribution to the expanding and critical discussion on nano-technoscience".[2]

Danny Heitman, in "Francis Bacon, Montaigne's Rival", informs that "Bacon wrote canonical essays, steeped in realism and insight, but his true legacy may rest with the sciences". The writings of Englishman Francis Bacon, an Elizabethan philosopher, statesman and pioneer of science, assess the relative obscurity of another English writer, the nineteenth-century essayist

---

[1] Giglioni G. "Philosophy according to Tacitus: Francis Bacon and the Inquiry into the Limits of Human Self-Delusion". Perspectives on Science, 2012, 20(2): 159-182.
[2] Schmidt J. "The Renaissance of Francis Bacon". NanoEthics, 2011(5): 29-41.

Charles Lamb. It is noted that Bacon seemed comfortable with often ruthlessly pragmatic worldview.①

2. Translation Study

Alan Stewart, in "Exporting Francis Bacon's *Essayes*", discusses Francis Bacon's several essays. Those essays were translated into Italian and French languages, and were received by local gentlemen with enthusiasm. The author also notes printer John Bill's decision to make surplus copies of some books.②

3. Rhetorical Study

Matthew Sharpe, in "Home to Men's Business and Bosoms: Philosophy and Rhetoric in Francis Bacon's *Essayes*", claims that today's reading of Francis Bacon's *Essayes* as a solely literary text turns upon philosophers' having largely lost access to the renaissance culture which Bacon inherited, and the renaissance debates about the role of rhetoric in philosophy in which Bacon participated. The article has two parts. Building upon Ronald Crane's seminal contribution on the place of the *Essayes* in Bacon's "great instauratio", Part 1 examines how the subjects of Bacon's *Essayes* need to be understood as Baconian contributions to "morrall philosophye" and "civile knowledge", rather than rhetorical or poetic exercises. In Part 2, contesting the interpretations of Crane, Fish, Ferrari and others, the author argues that *Essayes*' striking rhetorical form needs to be conceptualized in light of Bacon's renaissance account of the "duty and office" of rhetoric in any moral and civil philosophy that would look to actively cure mental afflictions and cultivate the virtuous or canny conduct it extols. Bacon's *Essayes*, in this light, are best understood as a legatee and transformation of the popular early modern genre of books of apothegms and maxims designed to guide conduct.③

4. Aesthetic Study

Jakub Zdebik Gail, and Stephen A. Jarislowsky, in "Skin Aesthetics as Incarnation: Gilles Deleuze's Diagram of Francis Bacon", present on Gilles Deleuze's treatment on the paintings of

---

① Heitman D. "Francis Bacon, Montaigne's Rival". Humanities, 2022, 43(2): 1.
② Stewart A. "Exporting Francis Bacon's *Essayes*". Shakespeare Studies, 2020(48): 94-100.
③ Sharpe M. "Home to Men's Business and Bosoms: Philosophy and Rhetoric in Francis Bacon's *Essayes*". British Journal for the History of Philosophy, 2019, 27(3): 492-512.

Francis Bacon according to his notion of skin aesthetics as incarnation. This paper describes some of Bacon's paintings including *Three Studies for Figures at the Base of a Crucifixion* and *Three Studies for a Crucifixion*. It also explores the concept of incarnation through analogy, essence, and virtual duality, citing the diagrammatical incarnation of a fish into a crucified body.[1]

5. Religious Study

Jeffrey Cordell, in "Baconian Apologetics: Knowledge and Charity in *The Advancement of Learning*", "examines the way in which Francis Bacon's *The Advancement of Learning* reflects arguments founded on Pauline notions of charity in the anti-Scholostic polemics of Christian humanists Thomas More and Juan Luis Vives". Emphasis is given to the influence of Christian humanism in Bacon's natural philosophy regarding evidence and knowledge directed towards charitable ends. Other topics include early Christian distinctions between false and true knowledge, the humanist critique of Scholasticism, and mediating between man and God.[2]

Sorana Corneanu, in "The Nature and Care of the Whole Man: Francis Bacon and Some Late Renaissance Contexts", argues that in the early seventeenth century, Francis Bacon called for the institution of a distinct field of theoretical and practical knowledge that would deal with the tight interrelationship between the mind and the body of man, which he dubbed "the inquirie tovching hvmane natvre entyre". According to Bacon, such knowledge was already in existence, but unfortunately scattered in medical and religious texts. As a remedy, he proposed an integrated and autonomous account that would constitute "one general science concerning the nature and state of man". Such an account would concern itself with both the nature of the bond (vinculum) between mind and body and with the medicalreligious care of man in his entirety. The author of this article tries to identify a number of late Renaissance contexts that flagged a comparable type of preoccupation with the nature, and care of the "whole man" from a perspective that similarly strove to combine philosophy, medicine and theology.[3]

Marta Fattori, in "Sir Francis Bacon and the Holy Office", gives an appendix with selected documents chosen from a list of thirty important documents found in and taken from the Archives of the Congregation for the Doctrine of the Faith (formerly the Holy Office, referred to as ACDF). "They all concern Francis Bacon and may be divided into two categories: the

---

[1] Gail J Z, Jarislowsky S A. "Skin Aesthetics as Incarnation: Gilles Deleuze's Diagram of Francis Bacon". English Studies in Canada, 2008, 34(1): 149-164.

[2] Cordell J. "Baconian Apologetics: Knowledge and Charity in *The Advancement of Learning*". Studies in Philology, 2011, 108(1): 86-107.

[3] Corneanu S. "The Nature and Care of the Whole Man: Francis Bacon and Some Late Renaissance Contexts". Early Science and Medicine, 2017(22): 130-156.

documents preceded by an asterisk have already been published by me and they are presented here for the first time translated into English; the second group appears in the original version with an English translation; many other documents for reference purposes are indicated in the footnotes, but they will all be published in a forthcoming book, *Sir Francis Bacon and the Holy Office*".[1]

6. Cultural Study

Rina Arya, in "Remaking the Body: The Cultural Dimensions of Francis Bacon", argues that "In 2008 the Tate Gallery hosted a retrospective of Francis Bacon to commemorate his centenary. This occasion was one of the motivations for presenting this reflection on Bacon and his legacy 16 years after his death. The exhibition demonstrated Bacon's technical ability to capture the nuances of flesh in a remarkably visceral way and consolidated his position as one of the greatest painters of the human body. In this article, I want to concentrate on the cultural dimensions of Bacon's weltanschauung. I argue that it is not a misrepresentation to discuss Bacon as a social and cultural commentator but rather a way of intensifying his aestheticism".[2]

Rina Arya, in "Constructions of Homosexuality in the Art of Francis Bacon", contextualizes Bacon's representations of homosexuality—that is, same-sex relations between men. The male nude made its appearance in Bacon's work in the early 1950s, a time when the nude was not a popular subject in painting and when, perhaps more critically, homosexuality was illegal in Britain. Other British contemporary homosexual artists, such as Robert Colquhoun and Robert MacBryde, steered clear of representing homosexuality, whilst others, such as Keith Vaughan, depicted homosexuality in their art in an ambiguous and diffuse fashion, often with recourse to the homoerotic. Vaughan's studies of men exercising focused on the strength and virility of the male nude, and were erotically charged without being overtly sexual. In contrast, Bacon chose to be more explicit in his depictions. He did not simply allude to, but pointed to the homosexual act of copulation. Given that Bacon was painting at a time before the legalisation of homosexuality, how can these images be explained and what was Bacon attempting to do? His representations of the homoerotic and homosexual convey social attitudes of the time and are important constructions and mediations of homosexual desire. The author of this article explains her motivations by drawing on Bacon's cultural and theoretical background. What is evident is that there is not one homogeneous interpretation of Bacon's depiction of homosexuality, but multiple readings, which are interdisciplinary. His depictions can be explained with recourse to his

---

[1] Fattori M. "Sir Francis Bacon and the Holy Office". British Journal for the History of Philosophy, 2005, 13(1): 21–49.
[2] Arya R. "Remaking the Body: The Cultural Dimensions of Francis Bacon". Journal for Cultural Research, 2009, 13(2): 143–158.

biography, art historical influences, political activism and his existential awareness of death. The author also demonstrates how changes in the political landscape affects Bacon's portrayals in the delineation of what she describes as four thematic phases in Bacon's art. [1]

7. Psychological Study

Silvia Manzo, in "Francis Bacon: Freedom, Authority and Science", discusses how Francis Bacon proposes to replace the older patterns of authority and freedom in science. It exposes the approach of Bacon to authority in theology, law and politics. The psychological aspects of the freedom of the scientist are offered. This article also discusses the authority in science, which is considered as an institution of the state and as an inquisition of nature. [2]

8. Linguistic Study

Kate Aughterson, in "Redefining the Plain Style: Francis Bacon, Linguistic Extension, and Semantic Change in *The Advancement of Learning*", argues that in *The Advancement of Learning*, the views of Francis Bacon on literary style and language differ from previous views in his works. Topics discussed include views of Bacon on representation; changes and adaptations of Bacon on semantic meanings; and how meaning is extended and restricted. [3]

9. Historical Study

Peter Harrison, in "Francis Bacon, Natural Philosophy, and the Cultivation of the Mind", suggests that "Bacon offers an Augustinian (rather than a purely Stoic) model of the 'culture of the mind'. He applies this conception to natural philosophy in an original way, and his novel application is informed by two related theological concerns. First, the Fall narrative provides a connection between the cultivation of the mind and the cultivation of the earth, both of which are seen as restorative of an original condition. Second, the fruit of the cultivation of the mind is the virtue of charity, which is understood not only as curing the mind of the individual, but as contributing to

---

[1] Arya R. "Constructions of Homosexuality in the Art of Francis Bacon". Journal for Cultural Research, 2012, 16(1): 43-61.

[2] Manzo S. "Francis Bacon: Freedom, Authority and Science". British Journal for the History of Philosophy, 2006, 14(2): 245-273.

[3] Aughterson K. "Redefining the Plain Style: Francis Bacon, Linguistic Extension, and Semantic Change in *The Advancement of Learning*". Studies in Philology, 2000, 97(1): 96-143.

human welfare and ameliorating some of the material losses that resulted from the Fall". [1]

Tom Lockwood, in " 'Empericks of State': Manuscript Verse and the Impeachment of Francis Bacon", discusses a case study both of the conceptual relations between public and private and the sociability of textual exchanges made possible in manuscript. It argues that a study of the poems on Francis Bacon's impeachment allow readers to place Bacon's household, its members and their shared textual economy within the dialogue between the public and private. This article notes that the distinction in the case of Bacon's impeachment was harder to maintain as his accusers sought to define.[2]

Jo Van Cauter, in "Wisdom as a Meditation on Life: Spinoza on Bacon and Civil History", discusses that "In letter 37 to Johannes Bouwmeester, Spinoza identifies a historiola mentisà la Bacon as an important tool for distinguishing more easily between adequate and inadequate ideas. This paper contends that Spinoza's advice is to take into account Baconian-style 'Civil History' as providing instructive material for contemplating the variety, complexity, and persistency of human passionate behaviour. Specifically, it argues that Baconian civil history forms an integral part of Spinoza's reflections on provisional morality. Although for Spinoza, philosophical beatitude ultimately demands understanding affects through their first causes—the intuitive perception of things sub specie aeternitatis—in the realm of everyday Spinoza allows for a different, more pragmatic approach to morality. This paper argues at this stage that a philosophical understanding of the mind and its affections is not needed. Spinoza, following Bacon, holds that conduct of practical affairs is particularly improved when those so engaged acquire historical knowledge of the human condition and apply it. Specifically, both authors place special emphasis on a history of men's characters, actions, and vices as providing the material basis for concrete, directly applicable moral and civil precepts". [3]

Anna-Maria Hartmann, in "Light from Darkness: The Relationship between Francis Bacon's Prima Philosophia and His Concept of the Greek Fable", argues that "Francis Bacon's *Great Instauration* was projected as a restoration of learning. At the end of it, mankind would have complete dominion over nature, after having re-established the knowledge Adam had before the fall. This knowledge was to be obtained by fresh research along the lines Bacon sketched in his oeuvre; it was not to be recovered from old books, from the darkness of the past. The Greek fables, however, were an apparent exception to this rule and their interpretation was declared a desideratum of the new philosophy. This article suggests an explanation for this exception. It

---

[1] Harrison P. "Francis Bacon, Natural Philosophy, and the Cultivation of the Mind". Perspectives on Science, 2012, 20(2): 139-158.

[2] Lockwood T. " 'Empericks of State': Manuscript Verse and the Impeachment of Francis Bacon". Philological Quarterly, 2012, 91(1): 23-47.

[3] Van Cauter J. "Wisdom as a Meditation on Life: Spinoza on Bacon and Civil History". British Journal for the History of Philosophy, 2015, 24(1): 1-23.

discovers an intimate connection between Bacon's concept of primary philosophy and his concept of parabolic poetry and argues that he might have hoped to find axioms of primary philosophy in the Greek fables".[①]

10. Biographical Study

Damian X. Powell, in "Why Was Sir Francis Bacon Impeached? The Common Lawyers and the Chancery Revisited: 1621", points out that "The relationship between legal debate and political dissent in the Jacobean era is open to question, and historians have disputed the effect of common law discourse upon political debate. In 1969 John Baker investigated the legal controversies between the common lawyer and the chancery that resulted in Sir Edward Coke's dismissal from the bench in 1616. Revising Maitland's confident estimation of a 'final and complete' victory for the chancery, Baker noted a declaration on the part of Chancellor Ellesmere's Successor, Sir Francis Bacon, not to subvert the law—concluding that with this assurance 'the bone of contention was buried'". Additional topics include peculiar circumstances surrounding Bacon's prosecution; Chancellor's impeachment as a way of demonstrating parliamentary displeasure with royal policy; and exposure of Bacon's corruption.[②]

11. Feminism Study

Brian Vickers, in "Francis Bacon, Feminist Historiography, and the Dominion of Nature", relates the reputations of English philosopher Francis Bacon in 1561-1626. "The history of ideas is an unstable business. Schools of thought are set up, fought over, and vanish... The reputations of philosophers, too, rise and fall irrationally, like the movements of stock markets. Perhaps no major figure has been subject to so many fluctuations as Francis Bacon". This article examines the fortune of his works in which according to the author has suffered against several individuals like the Voltaire and Diderot, Macaulay and De Maistre, Whewell and Spedding, L. C. Knights and Sandra Harding. The author also presents the allegation of the three female historian against Bacon and his Scientific Revolution by accusing that he has advocated the rape and torture of the nature.[③]

---

① Hartmann A-M. "Light from Darkness: The Relationship between Francis Bacon's Prima Philosophia and His Concept of the Greek Fable". The Seventeenth Century, 2011, 26(2): 203-220.
② Powell D X. "Why Was Sir Francis Bacon Impeached? The Common Lawyers and the Chancery Revisited: 1621". History, 1996, 81(264): 511-526.
③ Vickers B. "Francis Bacon, Feminist Historiography, and the Dominion of Nature". Journal of the History of Ideas, 2008, 69(1): 117-141.

Chapter 2
Jonathan Swift

Jonathan Swift (1667-1745)

Jonathan Swift was an Anglo-Irish author, who was the foremost prose satirist in the English language. Besides the celebrated novel *Gulliver's Travels* (1726), he wrote such shorter works as *A Tale of a Tub* (1704) and *A Modest Proposal* (1729). Swift's intellectual roots lay in the rationalism that was characteristic of late 17th-century England. This rationalism, with its strong moral sense, its emphasis on common sense, and its distrust of emotionalism, gave him the standards by which he appraised human conduct. At the same time, however, he provided a unique description of reason's weakness and of its use by people to delude themselves. His moral principles are scarcely original; his originality lies rather in the quality of his satiric imagination and his literary art. [1]

---

[1] https://www.britannica.com/biography/Jonathan-Swift.

Critical Perspectives

1. Postcolonial Study

Eoin Ó Cuinneagáin, in "The Darker Side of Jonathan Swift: On the Coloniality of Being in *A Modest Proposal* (1729)", reads *A Modest Proposal* from the darker side of the westernised/anglicised Enlightenment. Firstly, this article critically engages with the proclivity within the Anglocentric academy to celebrate English language literary figures associated with "The Enlightenment" in Ireland without a questioning of their role in the colonial project and in shaping its discourses of racism and sexism. Secondly, it focuses on how, from an Irish decolonial perspective, Jonathan Swift can be understood as a manager of the colonial racial/patriarchal matrix of power. Thirdly, it argues that the satire written by Jonathan Swift should be understood as an Anglocentric geo-cultural category and may be understood as westernised/anglicised Enlightenment satire. Finally, *A Modest Proposal* is analysed in terms of the exceptionality principle of irony, Swift's project of improvement and salvation of the colonised, and modernity/coloniality's rhetorical promise yet inability to solve the problems it produces.[1]

Sean Moore, in "The Irish Contribution to the Ideological Origins of the American Revolution: Nonimportation and the Reception of Jonathan Swift's Irish Satires in Early America", explores the Irish influence regarding boycott and protest against British imperial authority on the ideological development of the American Revolution. Emphasis is given to the writings of satirist Jonathan Swift and the dissemination of his work through the transatlantic book trade. Books noted include *A Proposal for the Universal Use of Irish Manufacture*, *Drapier's Letters*, and *A Modest Proposal*.[2]

Siyeon Lee, in "Colonial Discourse on Irish Dress and the Self as 'Outward Dress': Swift's Sartorial Self-Fashioning", presents that "Jonathan Swift's Irish writings are replete with sartorial imaginings that fashion his unique satirist self by interlacing, for mutual sub version, colonial discourse on Irish dress with a mock-Lockean idea of self as 'outward Dress'. Swift contests the legacy of Edmund Spenser's *A View of the State of Ireland* (ca. 1596), a colonial

---

[1] Cuinneagáin E Ó. "The Darker Side of Jonathan Swift: On the Coloniality of Being in *A Modest Proposal*(1729)". Estudios Irlandeses, 2023(18): 11-27.

[2] Moore S. "The Irish Contribution to the Ideological Origins of the American Revolution: Nonimportation and the Reception of Jonathan Swift's Irish Satires in Early America". Early American Literature, 2017, 52(2):333-362.

attack on Irish dress that combined the Renaissance notion of dress generating identity by permeating the wearer and a more modern presumption of essential differences between the Irish and (New) English. Swift's insight into Spenser's contradictory logic penetrates Jack's sartorial 'Projects of Separation' from Peter in *A Tale of a Tub* (1704), and culminates later in *Gulliver's Travels* (1726) and *A Modest Proposal* (1729) when Gulliver and the Modest Proposer, in deed or word, skin the Yahoos/Irish and literally turn them into shoes, in resonance with both William Wood's contumely 'eat [y]our Brogues' and Spenser's *View*. By reversing and revamping the colonial sign of Irish dress, Swift fashions and refashions his satirist self through a conscious mismatch of Anglican habit and Irish brogues". [1]

2. Narratology Study

David M. Palumbo, in "From 'Laughing' to 'Rayl[ing]' with a 'Few Friends': *A Modest Proposal* as Private Satire", presents an analysis of the essay *A Modest Proposal* by Jonathan Swift. It examines how the essay reflects Swift's personal views on the theory of satire, looking at how *A Modest Proposal* moved from public to private satire. Particular attention is given to Swift's personal life as the author argues that Swift has moved from associating with English friends to Irish friends due to backlash from his satire of English politics, making the satirization more private in nature. [2]

Katie Lanning, in "'Fitted to the Humour of the Age': Alteration and Print in Swift's *A Tale of a Tub*", suggests that alteration links seemingly disparate ideas and pieces of the text in Jonathan Swift's *A Tale of a Tub*. "In the *Tale*'s allegory, brothers alter their coats through over-embellishment. In the *Tale*'s digressions, the Grub Street narrator alters texts by overvaluing and reading only added commentary and prolegomena. The *Tale*'s material format also demonstrates surface alteration in its constant shifting between forms and in the changes Swift makes to the 1710 edition. Books and bodies alike are altered by layers of new surfaces in the *Tale*. Swift suggests that in both cases these exterior alterations possess the ability to disrupt and distort interiors, producing madness in bodies and misreading in books. Uneasy with the possibility of alterations unbalancing or destabilizing his meaning in an attempt to fit the text 'to the humour of the Age', Swift creates a work that possesses the potential to grow with material alteration. Any errors, additions, or changes to his text over time, even if Swift might despise them, validate his strategy". [3]

---

[1] Lee S. "Colonial Discourse on Irish Dress and the Self as 'Outward Dress': Swift's Sartorial Self-Fashioning". Eighteenth-Century Fiction, 2017, 29(3): 455-477.

[2] Palumbo D M. "From 'Laughing' to 'Rayl[ing]' with a 'Few Friends': *A Modest Proposal* as Private Satire". The Eighteenth Century: Theory and Interpretation, 2018, 59(3): 259-278.

[3] Lanning K. "'Fitted to the Humour of the Age': Alteration and Print in Swift's *A Tale of a Tub*". Eighteenth-Century Fiction, 2014, 26(4): 515-536.

3. Psychoanalytical Study

Ruth Salvaggio, in "Swift and Psychoanalysis, Language and Woman", presents a psychoanalytic criticism of Jonathan Swift. Topics discussed include Swift's preoccupation with anal rather than sexual matters; controversy about whether Swift was neurotic or healthy; and exploration of *Gulliver's Travels* in terms of its phallocentric system.[①]

Feargal Whelan, in "'No nation wanted it so much': Beckett, Swift and Psychiatric Confinement in Ireland", argues that "Samuel Beckett displays an interest in portraying figures normally regarded as insane within their communities, and who are frequently depicted interacting with institutions of mental care. Taking the representation of three asylums in three separate works, this paper aims to explore a developing and complicated meditation on the subjects of mental health and incarceration by the author. Beckett's recurring reference to Jonathan Swift and the constant presence of sexual anxiety in these narratives allows him to produce a nuanced critique of the development of modes of confinement in the emerging Irish state".[②]

4. Religious Study

Paul Neimann, in "Things Indifferent: Adiaphora, Superstition, and Religious Ideology in Swift's *A Tale of a Tub*", discusses the work of essayist Jonathan Swift, which includes adiaphora, superstition, and religious ideology. Topics include skeptical and authoritarian elements pointed out by author Daniel Eilon in Swift's politics and revolutionary modernism, author Sarah Ellenzweig's remarks of hypocrisy in Swift's attitude towards religion, and views on adiaphora developed from reformation efforts to recast devotional forms.[③]

5. Historical Study

Ashley Marshall, in "'Fuimus Torys': Swift and Regime Change, 1714–1718", points out that "Accounts of Swift's life in the months and years following Queen Anne's death (August

---

[①] Salvaggio R. "Swift and Psychoanalysis, Language and Woman". Women's Studies, 1988, 15(4): 417-434.

[②] Whelan F. "'No nation wanted it so much': Beckett, Swift and Psychiatric Confinement in Ireland". Estudios Irlandeses, 2019, 14 (2): 92-103.

[③] Neimann P. "Things Indifferent: Adiaphora, Superstition, and Religious Ideology in Swift's *A Tale of a Tub*". Modern Philology, 2017, 114 (4): 820-844.

1714) stress his melancholic acceptance of the new world of Hanoverian rule: however unhappy he was about Whig ascendancy, he was unequivocally supportive of the Hanoverian accession and resigned to the Tory collapse. The extant evidence, however, suggests that Swift's hopes for the Tory future died quite slowly and that his attitude toward the Hanoverian regime was not as conservative and innocuous as most scholars seem determined to believe. Though we have no reason to suppose that Swift was a committed Jacobite, neither are we wise to suppose that he was entirely innocent in his disaffection. Significantly, in autumn 1714 he transferred his allegiance from the Earl of Oxford to the Viscount Bolingbroke—in other words, from the moderate to the radical, from the man looking to join and temper a Whig ministry to the man wanting to challenge it. Swift's correspondence in this period is frequently partially coded, and many incriminating letters were evidently burned by Swift and his friends, which means that we will never fully know what Swift thought or wanted in the first years of George I's reign. But what is clear is that the dominant view of Swift's politics—'Old Whig' despite his being a Tory in religion—does not satisfactorily encapsulate his multifaceted response to regime change in 1714-16".[1]

Erin Mackie, in "Swift and Mimetic Sickness", presents literary criticism of the essay *A Modest Proposal* and the books *Gulliver's Travels* and *A Tale of a Tub* by Jonathan Swift. It examines Jonathan Swift's critiques of modernity, with a particular focus on the concept of mimesis as explored in the book *Mimesis and Alterity* by theorist Michael Taussig. Topics discussed include authorship, print culture, satire, and illness.[2]

---

[1] Marshall A. "'Fuimus Torys': Swift and Regime Change, 1714-1718". Studies in Philology, 2015, 112(3): 537-574.
[2] Mackie E. "Swift and Mimetic Sickness". The Eighteenth Century: Theory and Interpretation, 2013, 54(3): 359-373.

Chapter 3
Joseph Addison

Joseph Addison (1672-1719)

    Joseph Addison was educated at Charterhouse, where he was a classmate of Richard Steele, and at Oxford, where he became a distinguished classical scholar. His travels on the Continent from 1699 to 1703 were recorded in *Remarks on Several Parts of Italy*. Addison first achieved prominence with *The Campaign* (1704), an epic celebrating the victory of Marlborough at Blenheim. The poem was commissioned by Lord Halifax, and its great success resulted in Addison's appointment in 1705 as undersecretary of state and in 1709 as secretary to the lord lieutenant of Ireland. He also held a seat in Parliament from 1708 until his death.

    Addison's most enduring fame was achieved as an essayist. In 1710, he began his contributions to *The Tatler*, which Richard Steele had founded in 1709. He continued to write for successive publications. His contributions to several periodicals raised the English essay to a degree of technical perfection never before achieved and perhaps never since surpassed. In a prose style marked by simplicity, order, and precision, he sought to engage men's thoughts toward reason, moderation, and a harmonious life.[1]

---

[1] https://ccel.org/ccel/addison.

Critical Perspectives

1. Historical Study

    Katarzyna Kozak, in "Depicting a Political Rival: Evolution of Richard Steele's Essay Periodical Writing", discusses that "The period between the Glorious Revolution and the end of Queen Anne's reign was a time when political parties struggled with one another in order to create their own distinctive identity. The rivalry between Whigs and Tories defined the political situation in early eighteenth century Britain and laid the foundation for the development of the ministerial machine of propaganda aimed at discrediting opponents and justifying the policies of the government. The rhetoric adopted by the contemporary political writers included the reason-passion bias so inextricably associated with the philosophical background of the 'Age of Reason'. From this perspective, this article sets out to trace the evolution in Steele's journalistic productions (*The Spectator, The Englishman, The Reader*) and to delineate key changes in his strategies for achieving political goals and, at the same time, discredit his rival paper—*The Examiner*". Joseph Addison's several essays are discussed.[①]

    Amy Witherbee, in "The Temporality of the Public in *The Tatler* and *The Spectator*", explores themes of time and public arising from essays by Richard Steele and Joseph Addison in their respective British periodicals *The Tatler* and *The Spectator*. Other subjects considered include how developments in mathematics, especially in probability theory, led to changes in Britain's public finance, banking, insurance, and joint-stock investing.[②]

    Steve Pincus, in "Addison's Empire: Whig Conceptions of Empire in the Early 18th Century", discusses why Whigs consider the Treaty of Utrecht to be an imperial disaster. Contemporary scholarship makes this a difficult question to answer. Imperial historians insist that it was an imperial triumph, while political historians point that rough-and-tumble party politics was not about empire. This article aims to recover the rich intellectual history of party political debate about empire in the age of Anne. The author of this article suggests that "there

---

① Kozak K. "Depicting a Political Rival: Evolution of Richard Steele's Essay Periodical Writing". Brno Studies in English, 2020, 46(2): 195–209.
② Witherbee A. "The Temporality of the Public in *The Tatler* and *The Spectator*". The Eighteenth Century: Theory and Interpretation, 2010, 51(1/2): 173–192.

was bitter conflict between Tories who sought territorial empire based on South American mines, and Whigs who sought a manufacturing empire based on penetrating South American markets with British manufactures. The Sacheverell trial and its aftermath marked a turning point in British imperial policy". As a result, the Whigs felt betrayed, venting their anger in the immediate aftermath of the Hanoverian succession. [1]

Charles A. Knight, in "*The Spectator*'s Moral Economy", discusses the economic views of Joseph Addison and Richard Steele that were expressed in their periodical *The Spectator*. Topics discussed include political upbringing of Addison and Steele; connection of morality with economics; international aspects; class issues; and model proposed by Addison and Steele.[2]

Stuart Sherman, in "'The General Entertainment of My Life': *The Tatler*, *The Spectator*, and the Quidnunc's Cure", suggests that "The quidnunc—the news addict hooked on the latest dispatches—remained a figure of fun throughout the eighteenth century, partly because he functioned as a comic canary in the era's ever-expanding coal mine of periodically printed news. Richard Steele coined the term and, with his collaborator Joseph Addison, satirized the affliction in the pages of *The Tatler* and *The Spectator*. Each periodical, in its own way, proposed the theatre as the quidnunc's likeliest corrective and cure. The tactics by which they did so at once anticipate and rewire some powerful theories of performance and mediation: Peggy Phelan's on the primacy of presence; Michael Warner's on the distinctive temporalities—theatrical, periodical—inhabited by the early eighteenth century's emerging, overlapping publics; Walter Benjamin's on the different operations of 'absorption' triggered by the singular, aureate work of art and the mass-directed entertainments made possible (and prolific) by modern technologies of reproduction. The quidnunc's disorder is an obsession with the trivial, but Steele and Addison, over the course of their two papers, manage to spin from it an argument more momentous, about theatre, journalism, and time itself in Queen Anne's age of burgeoning information".[3]

2. Feminism Study

Erin Mackie, in "Lady Credit and the Strange Case of the Hoop-petticoat", focuses on the hoop-petticoat to study the culture in 18th century England. Topics discussed include Joseph Addison's opinion of the hoop-petticoat; femininity as represented by contemporary allegories

---

[1] Pincus S. "Addison's Empire: Whig Conceptions of Empire in the Early 18th Century". Parliamentary History, 2012, 31(1): 99-117.
[2] Knight C A. "*The Spectator*'s Moral Economy". Modern Philology, 1993, 91(2): 161-179.
[3] Sherman S. "'The General Entertainment of My Life': *The Tatler*, *The Spectator*, and the Quidnunc's Cure". Eighteenth-Century Fiction, 2015, 27(3/4): 343-371.

about credit; judging the hoop as antisexual and seeking to restore the woman's body to nature; and subversive fashion hoax against the metaphysics which support patriarchy.①

3. Formalist Study

Anthony Pollock, in "Formalist Cultural Criticism and the Post-Restoration Periodical", explains formalism in the post-Restoration periodicals of essayist Joseph Addison and Richard Steele. It states that the Addison and Steele's periodicals, which possess strong sense of political and cultural inquiry, are being neglected by rhetorical and literary critics. Authors Sean Latham and Robert Scholes noted that these essay periodicals should be viewed as coherent cultural literary objects because of their unique collaborative investigation. Literary attributes of the essayists are also given.②

4. Biographical Study

Stephen Miller, in "The Strange Career of Joseph Addison", examines the literary career of eighteenth-century English essayist Joseph Addison. It claims that Addison was a poet, playwright, travel writer, and opera librettist. It cites that Addison was admired by such personalities as writers David Hume, Adam Smith and Samuel Johnson. It states that Addison's reputation rapidly deteriorated due to attacks by Bonamy Dobrée and T. S. Eliot.③

5. Psychological Study

Joel P. Sodano, in "Uneasy Passions: *The Spectator*'s Divergent Interpretations of Locke's Theory of Emotion", discusses the relationship between the English philosopher John Locke's theory on emotions and the 1711–1712 English daily periodical *The Spectator*, developed by Joseph Addison and Richard Steele. An overview of Locke's book *An Essay concerning Human Understanding* is provided.④

---

① Mackie E. "Lady Credit and the Strange Case of the Hoop-petticoat".College Literature,1993, 20(2): 27–43.
② Pollock A. "Formalist Cultural Criticism and the Post-Restoration Periodical". Philological Quarterly, 2007, 86(3): 227–250.
③ Miller S. "The Strange Career of Joseph Addison". The Sewanee Review, 2014, 122(4): 650–660.
④ Sodano J P. "Uneasy Passions: *The Spectator*'s Divergent Interpretations of Locke's Theory of Emotion". The Eighteenth Century: Theory and Interpretation, 2017, 58(4): 449–467.

Chapter 4
Samuel Johnson

Samuel Johnson (1709-1784)

Samuel Johnson, the premier English literary figure of the mid and late 18th century, was a writer of exceptional range: a poet, a lexicographer, a translator, a journalist and essayist, a travel writer, a biographer, an editor, and a critic. His literary fame has traditionally—and properly—rested more on his prose than on his poetry. As a result, aside from his two verse satires (1738, 1749), which were from the beginning recognized as distinguished achievements, and a few lesser pieces, the rest of his poems have not in general been well known. Yet his biographer James Boswell noted correctly that Johnson's "mind was so full of imagery, that he might have been perpetually a poet." Moreover, Johnson wrote poetry throughout his life, from the time he was a schoolboy until eight days before his death, composing in Latin and Greek as well as English. His works include a verse drama, some longer serious poems, several prologues, many translations, and much light occasional poetry. Johnson is a poet of limited range, but within that range he is a poet of substantial talent and ability.[①]

[①] https://www.poetryfoundation.org/poets/samuel-johnson.

Critical Perspectives

1. Historical Study

  Agai M. Jock, in "Samuel Johnson's View about Oduduwa in Connection with the Origins of the Yoruba", discusses that "The most favourable explanation pertaining to the Yoruba origin is that of the Oduduwa tradition according to which he is the original ancestor of the Yoruba people. Although the Yorubas have reached a settlement on Oduduwa as their ancestor, they disagree on the origin of Oduduwa. Whilst some associated his origin with Mecca or Arabia, others say Egypt or Israel. Samuel Johnson, the most prominent writer of the Yoruba history, discussed various theories that pertained to the origin of Oduduwa. He argued that Oduduwa or the original ancestors of the Yoruba people were Coptic Christians. Writers of Yoruba history from the 20th and 21st centuries had continued to build upon Johnson's view of the Yoruba origin in connection with Oduduwa. This research is a study of the Yoruba and Johnson's perspectives of Oduduwa in connection with the Yoruba origins. The research elucidates the circumstances of Johnson's Christianisation of the Egyptian origin of the Yoruba". This article contributes to a distinct understanding of the origin of the Yoruba in connection with the identity and the personality of Oduduwa. Students of history and cultural studies will find this research of utmost benefit because it explains the origin of the Yoruba from the perspective of Samuel Johnson, the first Yoruba man to document extensively on the Yoruba history, language, its culture and its people in a single document or collection.[①]

  Chance David Pahl, in "Teleology in Samuel Johnson's *Rasselas*", discusses the book *Rasselas* by Samuel Johnson, with particular focus given to the theme of teleology and the author's assertion that the book is intended to promote Thomistic teleology over Aristotelian teleology. The philosophical journey undertaken by the characters is examined, and the religious nature of the work is explored.[②]

[①] Jock A M. "Samuel Johnson's View about Oduduwa in Connection with the Origins of the Yoruba". Hervormde Teologiese Studies, 2020,76(4): 1-8.
[②] Pahl C D. "Teleology in Samuel Johnson's *Rasselas*". Renascence, 2012, 64(3): 221-232.

2. Cultural Study

Rhys Kaminski-Jones, in "Floating in the Breath of the People: Ossianic Mist, Cultural Health, and the Creation of Celtic Atmosphere, 1760–1815", uses Samuel Johnson's characterization of Gaelic culture as an essentially airborne phenomenon as the starting point for a wide-ranging consideration of the links between atmospheric and Celtic discourses during the Romantic era. This period has been deemed foundational to the literary "appearance" of air and the conceptual formation of Celticity, but these two cultural phenomena have rarely been considered in tandem. Beginning with a discussion of the atmospheric ideas that underpin the Poems of Ossian's infamous mists, the essay argues that critics have largely ignored the complexity of Macpherson's medicalized ecologies of air. The essay then moves on to consider the development of comparable cloudy symbolism during the Welsh cultural revival of the 1790s, when overcast skies became an organising metaphor used to express the cultural benightedness of Wales. The often-unexamined cliché of "Celtic mistiness" is revealed as a vital metaphor for the allure and imperfection of intercultural mediation.[①]

William Ferguson, in "Samuel Johnson's Views on Scottish Gaelic Culture", presents Samuel Johnson's views on Scottish Gaelic culture as reflected in his book *A Journey to the Western Islands of Scotland*. Topics discussed include assessment of Gaelic Scotland as devoid of culture and destitute of learning, and refutation of Johnson's view of Gaelic illiteracy by Donald McNicol's book *Remarks on Dr. Samuel Johnson's Journey to the Hebrides*.[②]

Howard D. Weinbrot, in "Samuel Johnson's Practical Sermon on Marriage in Context: Spousal Whiggery and the Book of Common Prayer", examines the practical sermon of author Samuel Johnson on marriage. Topics discussed include an overview of the sermons of Johnson; his achievements within the genre of sermons; the political aspects of his sermons; the writing of the sermons; and the sale and collection of these sermons.[③]

George P. Rice, in "Samuel Johnson, LL. D., on Law, Lawyers, and Judges", focuses on writer and literary critic Samuel Johnson's interest in the profession of law in Great Britain. Topics discussed include Johnson's attempts to enter the profession; James Boswell's writings on Johnson and his legal views; and Johnson's influence on British law.[④]

---

① Kaminski-Jones R. "Floating in the Breath of the People: Ossianic Mist, Cultural Health, and the Creation of Celtic Atmosphere, 1760–1815". Romanticism, 2021, 27(2): 135–148.
② Ferguson W. "Samuel Johnson's Views on Scottish Gaelic Culture". The Scottish Historical Review, 1998(77):183–198.
③ Weinbrot H D. "Samuel Johnson's Practical Sermon on Marriage in Context: Spousal Whiggery and the Book of Common Prayer". Modern Philology, 2016,114(2): 310–336.
④ Rice G P. "Samuel Johnson, LL. D., on Law, Lawyers, and Judges". American Bar Association Journal, 1977, 63(9): 1217–1219.

3. Narrative Study

Keith Stewart, in "Samuel Johnson and the Ocean of Life: Variations on a Commonplace", examines some of the uses to which writer Samuel Johnson put the commonplace of life as a voyage, the means by which he gave it variety and the distinction to which his own mind gave the usual formula. Topics discussed include elements of the ocean voyage as a metaphor for life; favorite metaphor of Johnson; images of uncertainty and distress included in Johnson's work *The Rambler*.[①]

Lisa Berglund, in "Allegory in *The Rambler*", traces the allegorical works made by Samuel Johnson at *The Rambler* periodical. Topics discussed include how Johnson defines the term allegory; observation of Johnson on the poem *Absalom and Achitopel*; types of papers characterized by Johnson's retrospective analysis of the periodical; interpretation on the allegorical histories written by Johnson for the periodical; and root of the differences between Wolfgang Iser's analysis and Johnson's theory and practice of didactic fiction.[②]

Charles A. Knight, in "The Writer as Hero in Johnson's Periodical Essays", examines how the writer is depicted in the periodical essays of Samuel Johnson. Topics discussed include moral themes which dominate Johnson's periodical essays; reason for Johnson's conscious and dramatic avoidance of the traditional figure of the writer; and description of the writer according to Johnson.[③]

4. Philosophical Study

Geoffrey Gorham, in "Early American Immaterialism: Samuel Johnson's Emendations of Berkeley", analyzes Berkeley's correspondence during his American sojourn of 1729–1731 with the Connecticut philosopher and theologian Samuel Johnson, an early and influential convert to Berkeleianism. Although these letters have been examined by eminent Berkeley scholars including Jessop, Luce, and Popkin, their treatments of Johnson are not charitable. Contrary to Luce, who asserts that Johnson is "muddled" on several points, and "strikes at the root" of Berkeley's philosophy, "I maintain that Johnson offers plausible and friendly amendments to Berkeley's system—concerning (i) archetypes; (ii) space and duration; (iii) the esse of finite

---

① Stewart K. "Samuel Johnson and the Ocean of Life: Variations on a Commonplace". Papers on Language and Literature, 1987, 23(3): 305–317.
② Berglund L. "Allegory in *The Rambler*". Papers on Language and Literature, 2001, 37(2):147–178.
③ Knight C A. "The Writer as Hero in Johnson's Periodical Essays". Papers on Language and Literature, 1977, 13(3): 238–250.

spirits—which would help to reconcile Berkeley with Newtonian natural philosophy and with common sense".①

5. Psychological Study

Stephen John Dilks, in "Samuel Becktt's Samuel Johnson", discusses how the development of a selective portrait of author Samuel Johnson by Samuel Beckett helps him begin to articulate his own literary aesthetic. Topics discussed include the analysis of the period of preparation made by Samuel Johnson, and reconstruction of the relationship between Samuel Beckett and James Joyce before and after 1937.②

6. Biographical Study

Stephen Miller, in "Why Read Samuel Johnson?", focuses on the conflicting opinions of Samuel Johnson's merits among the classic English writers. Topics discussed include praises and attacks made by members of his club; Johnson's reputation of being a better speaker than a writer; unflattering portrait of Johnson in James Boswell's biography *Life of Johnson*; conflicts stirred by Johnson's outspoken nature; criticisms on British laws and policies; and political views.③

Anthony W. Lee, in "Sameul Johnson as Intertextual Critic", analyzes the critical outlook of Samuel Johnson, an author and literary critic, through intertextuality. It notes that mentoring and intertextuality are the factors vital to his literary and critical success. The analysis aims to establish Johnson's status as a major intertextual critic, analyze his use of mottos and translations from the periodical essays, and study the relationship between his intertextual practice and preoccupation with mentoring. It also aims to prove that intertextuality brings to light the nature of his critical work.④

Henrik Bering, in "The Ultimate Literary Portrait", details the friendship between James Boswell and English author Samuel Johnson. The focus is on information from Boswell's biography of Johnson, *The Journal of a Tour to the Hebrides*. Johnson's personal habits, physical description, poor eyesight, emotional demeanor, and opinions about people such as William Hogarth are mentioned.⑤

---

① Gorham G. "Early American Immaterialism: Samuel Johnson's Emendations of Berkeley". Transactions of the Charles S. Peirce Society, 2018, 54(4): 441-456.
② Dilks S J. "Samuel Beckett's Samuel Johnson". The Modern Language Review, 2003, 98(2): 285-298.
③ Miller S. "Why Read Samuel Johnson?". The Sewanee Review, 1999, 107(1): 44-60.
④ Lee A W. "Sameul Johnson as Intertextual Critic". Texas Studies in Literature and Language, 2010, 52(2): 129-156.
⑤ Bering H. "The Ultimate Literary Portrait". Policy Review, 2008(149): 61-74.

Bryan A. Garner, in "A 'Conversation' with the Late, Great Lexicographer Samuel Johnson", presents a mock conversational interview with the late lexicographer Samuel Johnson by utilizing Johnson's books which address his views about lawyers, the legal profession, and writings by attorneys. The study of law is examined, using a letter that Johnson sent to biographer James Boswell in 1766. Human wisdom and the relationship between law and dishonesty are examined, along with false reasoning and the late lawyers Francis Bacon and Judge Matthew Hale.[①]

Daniels Anthony, in "A Shared Wretchedness", examines the logic and philosophy of the eighteenth-century authors Jonathan Swift and Samuel Johnson. Particular focus is given to how Swift and Johnson often criticized the times and the world in which they lived. Johnson's attitude towards Swift is explored. The author of this article also studies Johnson's *Life of Swift*, which was published in the book *Lives of the English Poets*.[②]

Helen Deutsch, in " 'The Name of an Author': Moral Economics in Johnson's *Life of Savage*", describes the means by which Samuel Johnson, author of *An Account of the Life of Mr. Richard Savage, Son of the Earl Rivers*, sets the groundwork for his transformation into a paragon of authorship. Topics discussed include origin of Johnson's mode of authorship; exposition of the rhetorical basis of any claim; and conflict between particular fallible human examples and general rules of profitable conduct.[③]

James L. Battersby, in "Johnson's Negative Capability: Remarks on Omissions from the Canon", attempts to show that certain forms of writing fall outside the range of tolerance constituted by the principles of English writer Samuel Johnson. Topics discussed include types of works lacking representation in the Johnsonian canon, and reasons for Johnson's neglect of the types.[④]

---

① Garner B A. "A 'Conversation' with the Late, Great Lexicographer Samuel Johnson". ABA Journal, 2016,102(3): 1.
② Anthony D. "A Shared Wretchedness". The New Criterion, 2010, 28(9): 10-15.
③ Deutsch H. " 'The Name of an Author': Moral Economics in Johnson's *Life of Savage*". Modern Philology, 1995, 92(3): 328-345.
④ Battersby J L. "Johnson's Negative Capability: Remarks on Omissions from the Canon". Papers on Language and Literature,1980, 16(2): 151-160.

Chapter 5
Charles Lamb

Charles Lamb (1775-1834)

  Essayist, critic, poet, and playwright Charles Lamb achieved lasting fame as a writer during the years 1820–1825, when he captivated the discerning English reading public with his personal essays in *The London Magazine*, collected as *Essays of Elia* (1823) and *The Last Essays of Elia* (1833). Known for their charm, humor, and perception, and laced with idiosyncrasies, these essays appear to be modest in scope, but their soundings are deep, and their ripples extend to embrace much of human life—particularly the life of the imagination. In the 20th century, Lamb was also recognized for his critical writings; *Lamb as Critic* (1980) gathers his criticism from all sources, including letters.[1]

---

[1] https://www.poetryfoundation.org/poets/charles-lamb.

Critical Perspectives

1. Narrative Study

Eliza Haughton-Shaw, in "Charles Lamb's Imperfect Solitudes", presents that "Charles Lamb's *Essays of Elia* (1820-25) are often seen as minor contributions to the Romantic tradition, and the essays themselves playfully foreground their own minority. This article traces the self-deprecating humour of the Elia essays to the writer's perceived inability to generate for himself the kind of self-enclosure which is envisioned by the Romantic lyric. It reads solitude as both a wished-for state and a concept under formation in the Elia writings, and argues that humour—with its masks, alternate selves, and performance of roles—offers Lamb an alternative to the more serious authority of Wordsworth and Coleridge, and a way of 'making do' with imperfect environmental conditions for creativity".[1]

Christopher S. Nield, in "Distant Correspondents: Charles Lamb, Exploration and the Writing of Letters", examines Charles Lamb's relationships with the travelers Barron Field and Thomas Manning. Scheme by which the ideas of the status of the explorer and the difficulties of international correspondence are brought together within an analysis of Romantic sociability. Topics discussed inlcude materiality of communication; ideologies of presence that govern the mechanisms of coterie formation; and ways in which international letters haunt Romantic coteries with images of friendship.[2]

Janet Bottoms, in "The Battle of the (Children's) Books", explores varying opinions and reasoning behind what is "proper reading" for children in the 19th century. The author particularly gives a defense of the fantasy genre. An overview of the different influential groups and individuals in the defining of juvenile literature is given, such as the philosophy of John Locke and the writings of Charles Lamb, along with suggested implications on the common view of the genre in modern times.[3]

---

[1] Haughton-Shaw E. "Charles Lamb's Imperfect Solitudes". Romanticism, 2022, 28(3): 233-245.
[2] Nield C S. "Distant Correspondents: Charles Lamb, Exploration and the Writing of Letters". Romanticism, 2004, 10(1): 79-94.
[3] Bottoms J. "The Battle of the (Children's) Books". Romanticism, 2006, 12(3): 212-222.

2. Psychological Study

Michael J. Kraus, in "The Greatest Rock Star of the 19th Century: Ray Davies, Romanticism, and the Art of Being English", considers Ray Davies in the context of the English Romantic art tradition. By connecting Davies with Romantics like William Wordsworth, John Keats, William Blake, and Charles Lamb, this essay explores Davies's language, characterizations, themes, development of a personal mythology, use of antitheses, and sense of "negative capability". The influence of the English art school on Davies is also explored.[①]

3. Historical Study

David Higgins, in "Imagining the Exotic: De Quincey and Lamb in *The London Magazine*", discusses the contributions of British authors Charles Lamb and Thomas De Quincey to *The London Magazine* in the 1820s. The article focuses upon the October 1821 issue of *The London Magazine*, in which both Lamb and De Quincey published articles about exotic consumption and imagination. It examines Lamb's and De Quincey's writings on the exotic aspects of foreign culture. The article discusses Lamb's experiences as a clerk with the East India Company and its influence on his writing and his thoughts on British imperialism.[②]

Hazel Mackenzie, in "The Discipline of Sympathy and the Limits of Omniscience in Nineteenth-Century Journalism", presents that nineteenth-century literary journalism is often read in the light of Michel Foucault's disciplinary paradigm as articulated in his seminal work *Discipline and Punish: The Birth of the Prison*. "Contextualising the growth of literary journalism within the evolution of the modern, urban society, this article explores the ways in which journalists in this period manipulated generic conventions to both enact and resist their role in creating a more transparent, disciplined society. Looking at the journalism of Charles Lamb, William Hazlitt, Charles Dickens, Charles Collins, John Hollingshead and William Makepeace Thackeray, this article will argue that their use of a limited, first-person perspective and their emphasis on feeling and sympathy attempts to resist a passive and disciplinary spectatorship and yet paradoxically it is the most significantly disciplinary aspect of their texts".[③]

---

① Kraus M J. "The Greatest Rock Star of the 19th Century: Ray Davies, Romanticism, and the Art of Being English". Popular Music and Society, 2006, 29(2): 201-212.
② Higgins D. "Imagining the Exotic: De Quincey and Lamb in *The London Magazine*". Romanticism, 2011, 17(3): 288-298.
③ Mackenzie H. "The Discipline of Sympathy and the Limits of Omniscience in Nineteenth-Century Journalism". Critical Survey, 2014, 26(2): 53-72.

4. Religious Study

Gurion Taussig, in "'Lavish Promises': Coleridge, Charles Lamb and Charles Lloyd, 1794–1798", explores the religious language which persistently gathers around discussions of the friendships of 18th century Romance writers Samuel Taylor Coleridge, Charles Lamb and Charles Lloyd. Topics discussed include construction of friendship in religious terms; religious idealism that clashed with the writers' practical experience of friendship; and conflict between spiritual and worldly conceptions of friendship.[1]

Duncan Wu, in "The Lamb Circle and *The Monthly Repository*", presents a look at the periodical *The Monthly Repository*, which the author suggests is associated with the Romantic essayist Charles Lamb. Lamb's association with the Unitarian of the Priestleyan stripe in the 1790s is also discussed. The author provides further biographical information regarding Lamb's social, political and religious involvement.[2]

---

[1] Taussig G. "'Lavish Promises': Coleridge, Charles Lamb and Charles Lloyd, 1794–1798". Romanticism, 2000, 6(1): 78–97.

[2] Wu D. "The Lamb Circle and *The Monthly Repository*". Romanticism, 2006, 12(2): 143–149.

Chapter 6
William Hazlitt

William Hazlitt (1778-1830)

  William Hazlitt was an English writer best known for his humanistic essays. Lacking conscious artistry or literary pretention, his writing is noted for the brilliant intellect it reveals. Early in his career he worked briefly as a portraitist, but he lived mainly by journalism, writing for numerous newspapers and journals. He was a Romantic in outlook, placing more importance on the role of genius in artistic creation than on rules or theories. Thus he admired Reynolds's paintings, but attacked his ideas. A notable feature of Hazlitt's writing is that (unlike most previous art criticism) it was written for the general reader rather than for the connoisseur or practising artist.[1]

---

[1] https://www.britannica.com/biography/William-Hazlitt.

Critical Perspectives

1. Narrative Study

Cristina Consiglio, in "The London Theatre Scene in William Hazlitt's Dramatic Criticism", focuses on English literary critic William Hazlitt's interpretation of theater scene in London, England, with special reference to playwright William Shakespeare's work. The topics discussed includes focus of Hazlitt's lectures and articles on theater; investigation of the nature of Shakespeare's characters; and the style of the actors.[①]

Jaspreet S. Tambar, in "Hazlitt and the Tradition of the Characteristic", argues that William Hazlitt has had the flattering misfortune of being celebrated as one of the greatest essayists in England, and his literary heritage was limited to the British Isles. "Further, the genre of his fame has sometimes led critics to view his writings as Turner did the coastal seas—impressionistic and occasionally glittering with illumination. However, I argue that Hazlitt is an important heir of and contributor to the Swiss-German theory of the characteristic, which he consistently, if not programmatically, pursues throughout the gamut of his works. The characteristic is a concept of aesthetic semblance first articulated by Aloys Hirt, and then by such figures as Goethe and Henry Fuseli, that straddles the classical and romantic movement, and Hazlitt receives it from Fuseli. The characteristic—of which portraiture, because of its relation to sympathetic representation, is for Hazlitt the highest symbol—is in fact a defining feature of Hazlitt's aesthetics and connects him to the major art-theoretical figures of European Romanticism".[②]

Marcus Tomalin, in "'Vulgarisms and Broken English': The Familiar Perspicuity of William Hazlitt", examines the use of colloquial and vernacular English in early 19th century Romantic literature as a distinct literary style. The author focuses on the writings of William Hazlitt and his literary aesthetics, pointing out the writer's choice to manifest a "familiar" style of writing for an artistic and intellectual end, rather than simply evidence flaws of the text. Hazlitt's essay *On Familiar Style* is explored in depth.[③]

---

① Consiglio C. "The London Theatre Scene in William Hazlitt's Dramatic Criticism". Journal of the Wooden O, 2017(16): 86-94.
② Tambar J S. "Hazlitt and the Tradition of the Characteristic". Studies in Philology, 2018, 115(4): 835-856.
③ Tomalin M. "'Vulgarisms and Broken English': The Familiar Perspicuity of William Hazlitt". Romanticism, 2007, 13(1): 28-52.

David Halpin, in "Education, Criticism and the Creative Imagination: The legacy of William Hazlitt", discusses that "William Hazlitt (1778–1830), one of the most important critics of the English Romantic Period, held and published highly developed views about the nature of the creative imagination, the function of criticism and what it means to be truly learned. Although he never advanced an explicit theory of education, least of all one about the purposes of schooling, his principles of thought and action and his thesis about style and structure in writing are highly relevant to contemporary discussions of what counts as genuine learning and teaching and the intellectual vocation of members of the educational academy".①

Duncan Wu, in " 'Polemical Divinity': William Hazlitt at the University of Glasgow", discusses the place of Unitarianism in the writing of 19th century Romantic author William Hazlitt. Topics discussed include how Hazlitt's entire theory of imaginative thought is founded on Unitarian premises; question on how Hazlitt's father might have been moved to convert to Unitarianism at the University of Glasgow; and conflation of father's recollections of Glasgow with memories of his own mentor at the Hackney Academy.②

John Atkinson, in "Coriolanus, Hazlitt and the Insolence of Power", presents that "William Hazlitt's 1816 essay on Shakespeare's Coriolanus was supposedly a review of a production by John Kemble. Yet it begins with a reference to Burke and Paine, and develops as a discourse on republic versus monarchy. This would have been more appropriate if Shakespeare had based his play on the account of Dionysius of Halicarnassus, but Shakespeare took his material from Plutarch's life of Coriolanus, and Plutarch had recast Dionysius' account, since he was writing biography and not political history. Hazlitt used his essay to advance his campaign against contemporary poets, especially those of a Tory persuasion, and to vent his spleen against those who had abandoned their rational republican ideals in favour of celebrating the reinstatement of the monarchy in France and the defeat and humiliation of Napoleon".③

David Halpin, in "Hazlitt's Contrariness and Familiar Prose Style: Lessons on How to Be Critical", argues that contrariness of the kind manifest in the literary output and general disposition of the nineteenth century English essayist and journalist, William Hazlitt, has much to teach contemporary intellectuals working in the academy about how better to be critical, offering important lessons on the necessity for self-consistency and independence of thought and the need more to write for publication in a familiar and accessible conversational style.④

David Higgins, in "Englishness, Effeminacy, and the *New Monthly Magazine*: Hazlitt's The

---

① Halpin D. "Education, Criticism and the Creative Imagination: The legacy of William Hazlitt". London Review of Education, 2004, 2(1): 17–31.
② Wu D. " 'Polemical Divinity': William Hazlitt at the University of Glasgow". Romanticism, 2000, 6(2): 163–177.
③ Atkinson J. "Coriolanus, Hazlitt and the Insolence of Power". Shakespeare in Southern Africa, 2015(27): 15–23.
④ Halpin D. "Hazlitt's Contrariness and Familiar Prose Style: Lessons on How to Be Critical". London Review of Education, 2011, 9(3): 293–303.

Fight in Context", offers a reading of the essay *The Fight*, by the English essayist William Hazlitt. It is considered in three related contexts: firstly, the rhetoric and practice of prizefighting in Regency England; secondly, Hazlitt's infatuation with Sarah Walker, the daughter of his landlord; and thirdly, the circumstances of the essay's original publication in the *New Monthly Magazine* early in 1822. Published pseudonymously under the name Phantastes, *The Fight* is a literary performance that is both self-defining and self-effacing.①

Jeffrey C. Robinson, in "Hazlitt's *My First Acquaintance with Poets*: The Autobiography of a Cultural Critic", discusses the essay *My First Acquaintance with Poets*, which recounts William Hazlitt's response to radical poetics embodied in William Wordsworth and Samuel Taylor Coleridge. Topics discussed include self-representation of a neophyte enthusiast in philosophy and arts; argument that the essay is more than elegy and nostalgia followed by skepticism; and visionary poetics of the post-French Revolution period.②

2. Thematic Study

Jane Moore, in "Modern Manners: Regency Boxing and Romantic Sociability", presents an examination into the connections shared between the 19th-century English writers William Hazlitt and Mary Wollstonecraft. Focus is given to Hazlitt's 1822 essay *The Fight*, analyzed as a portrayal of masculine manners through the character of the boxer. Parallels are then made between Hazlitt's depiction of middle class masculinity and Wollstonecraft's parallel views and depictions of femininity.③

Danny Heitman, in "Partisan Principles", discusses political partisanship through heavily referencing the 1830 essay *On Party Spirit*, by English writer William Hazlitt. Topics discussed include political culture, the relationship between toleration and intolerance, pride and the emotional and moral aspects of partisanship.④

3. Religious Study

John Barresi, and Raymond Martin, in "Self-concern from Priestley to Hazlitt", present that "Toward the beginning of the nineteenth century, William Hazlitt, in his book *An Essay on the*

---

① Higgins D. "Englishness, Effeminacy, and the *New Monthly Magazine*: Hazlitt's *The Fight* in Context". Romanticism, 2004, 10(2): 173-190.
② Robinson J C. "Hazlitt's *My First Acquaintance with Poets*: The Autobiography of a Cultural Critic". Romanticism, 2000, 6(2): 178-194.
③ Moore J. "Modern Manners: Regency Boxing and Romantic Sociability". Romanticism, 2013, 19(3): 273-290.
④ Heitman D. "Partisan Principles". Phi Kappa Phi Forum, 2019, 99(2): 36.

Principles of Human Action, proposed a theory of personal identity and self-concern. Hazlitt even asked in regard to possible resurrection fission scenarios, how he could decide which of the multiple copies of himself or of his continued consciousness that were created by God were really himself or a proper object of his egoistic self concern. Hazlitt concluded that belief in personal identity must be an acquired imaginary conception".[1]

4. Feminism Study

John Derbyshire, in "Hazlitt's Philocaption: A Very Child in Love", provides information about William Hazlitt's philocaption. It is an inordinate love of one person for another. His philocaption could not have come to him as a complete surprise. He was chronically susceptible to infatuations with women much below himself in class and intellect.[2]

5. Historical Study

Brian Brivati, in "Michael Foot: A Hazlitt for Our Age?", presents a profile of the 20th-century British Labour Party politician Michael Foot and a comparison between him and the early 19th-century essayist William Hazlitt. Brief overviews of each figure are given, noting their similarities as influential and persuasive public figures regarding radical politics, their mutually high level of craftsmanship used in political writing, and their mutual love of literary criticism.[3]

---

[1] Barresi J, Martin R. "Self-concern from Priestley to Hazlitt". British Journal for the History of Philosophy, 2003, 11(3): 499-507.
[2] Derbyshire J. "Hazlitt's Philocaption: A Very Child in Love". The New Criterion, 2008, 27(2): 10-15.
[3] Brivati B. "Michael Foot: A Hazlitt for Our Age?". History Today, 2010, 60(5): 4-5.

Chapter 7
Thomas De Quincey

Thomas De Quincey (1785-1859)

Thomas De Quincey was an English essayist and critic, best known for his *Confessions of an English Opium-Eater*. The avowed purpose of the first version of the *Confessions* is to warn the reader of the dangers of opium, and it combines the interest of a journalistic exposé of a social evil, told from an insider's point of view, with a somewhat contradictory picture of the subjective pleasures of drug addiction. The book begins with an autobiographical account of the author's addiction, describes in detail the euphoric and highly symbolic reveries that he experienced under the drug's influence, and recounts the horrible nightmares that continued use of the drug eventually produced. The highly poetic and imaginative prose of the *Confessions* makes it one of the enduring stylistic masterpieces of English literature.[1]

---

[1] https://www.britannica.com/biography/Thomas-De-Quincey.

Critical Perspectives

1. Biographical Study

Roxanne Covelo, in "Thomas De Quincey in the Essays of Virginia Woolf: 'Prose Poetry' and the Autobiographic Mode", presents that British author Thomas De Quincey makes brief but frequent appearances in Virginia Woolf's essays of literary criticism, in which she examines what she understands to be their shared aesthetic objectives in the areas of prose-style and (auto)biographic writing. Interestingly, although Woolf often frames these objectives in terms that may be called post- or even anti-Victorian, her approach to De Quincey's work is strongly mediated by the critical scholarship of her father, the Victorian critic and biographer Leslie Stephen, and his own essays on De Quincey published between 1869 and 1927.[1]

Danielle Dutton, in "One Woman and Two Great Men", focuses on a glimpse of philosopher's bedtime routine given by the little-known drama The Last Days of Immanuel Kant, which is based on an essay by Thomas De Quincey. Topics discussed include the relationship between quotation and citation of De Quincey, words and experiences of De Quincey, and De Quincey's liberal curiosity.[2]

Robert Morrison, in "De Quincey's Addiction", presents a discussion of the drug and alcohol addictions of British essayist Thomas De Quincey. Most ideas of this article are taken from the book *The English Opium-Eater: A Biography of Thomas De Quincey* by Robert Morrison.[3]

2. Psychological Study

Gerald Maa, in "Thomas De Quincey's Stage-Work: Theater, Reading, Body, Affect", talks about a growing number of studies that find in the work of Thomas De Quincey's major contributions to the general practices, values, and blind spots of literary criticism in the

---

[1] Covelo R. "Thomas De Quincey in the Essays of Virginia Woolf: 'Prose Poetry' and the Autobiographic Mode". Journal of Modern Literature, 2018, 41(4): 31-47.
[2] Dutton D. "One Woman and Two Great Men". Chicago Review, 2021, 64/65(4-1): 124-128.
[3] Morrison R. "De Quincey's Addiction". Romanticism, 2011, 17(3): 270-277.

twentieth and twenty-first centuries. In particular, this essay argues that he aspires to create an embodied reading practice by underwriting his general theory of literature with his writings on drama. De Quincey values the theater as a place for phenomenal effect, and his literary criticism attempts to formulate a mode of textuality that can replicate, or at least approximate, the material effects of stage-work, thereby implicating the reader's perceptive body in the reading process. He, however, arrives at the impasse between the sensorial body and literature, an aesthetic medium completely mediated from the empirical world. In order to make the sensitized body the primary target of literature, De Quincey has to invent an interior space that obviates the problem that the body puts to reading, and he calls this the "subconscious". This essay demonstrates how De Quincey creates his literary theory of dramatic writing in conversation with William Wordsworth, Samuel Taylor Coleridge, and contemporary discourses about the stage. It also proposes that De Quincey fashions a formative critical practice that enlists techniques of the stage to sensitize and spatialize the reader's body. The problems, inventions, and solutions that he discovers prove that embodied reading can be possible only when supplemented by a notion of depth psychology.[1]

Markus Iseli, in "Thomas De Quincey's Subconscious: Nineteenth-Century Intimations of the Cognitive Unconscious", explores the use of the cognitive psychology term "subconscious" within the literary writings of the 19th-century English author Thomas De Quincey. Details are given explaining how De Quincey first coined the term in 1834. An overview is given of De Quincey's various uses of the concept throughout his literary and historical essays. Additional discussion is given contrasting De Quincey's subconscious concept with the technical psychoanalytical theory of Sigmund Freud and others.[2]

Robert Maniquis, in "De Quincey, Varieties of the Palimpsest, and the Unconscious", discusses the palimpsest *Suspiria de Profundis* by 19th century British essayist Thomas De Quincey. It examines the themes of memory, transcendent ego, and the metaphor of inscription. The article also discusses the Romantic aspect of the unconscious among pre-Romantic era authors. It also examines the literary device of memory among poets such as John Keats, Robert Frost, and William Wordsworth. The article discusses Freudian unconscious and the concept of belief in God among Romantic authors.[3]

Robert Morrison, in "De Quincey and the Opium-Eater's Other Selves", focuses on fictive constructs in Thomas De Quincey's *Confessions of an English Opium-Eater*. Topics discussed include interest in the rhetorical manipulation of identity and character; De Quincey's

---

[1] Maa G. "Thomas De Quincey's Stage-Work: Theater, Reading, Body, Affect". Criticism, 2018, 60(3): 341-361.
[2] Iseli M. "Thomas De Quincey's Subconscious: Nineteenth-Century Intimations of the Cognitive Unconscious". Romanticism, 2014, 20(3): 294-305.
[3] Maniquis R. "De Quincey, Varieties of the Palimpsest, and the Unconscious". Romanticism, 2011, 17(3): 309-318.

fascination with pseudonyms and the manufacturing of identity; fictionalization of identity; and creation of the Opium-Eater in the image of poet Samuel Taylor Coleridge.①

Warren Oakley, in "Physical Encounters as a Point of Contact between Sterne's *Journey* and De Quincey's *Confessions*", presents literary criticism of the books *A Sentimental Journey through France and Italy* by Laurence Sterne and *Confessions of an English Opium-Eater* by Thomas De Quincey. Particular focus is given to the influence of Sterne's book on De Quincey's depiction of travel through London, England. Details on literary appropriation and the effects of childhood reading on later autobiographical narratives are presented.②

3. Narrative Study

Robert Morrison, in "'Two faces, each of a confused countenance': Coleridge, De Quincey, and Contests of Authority", presents that Thomas De Quincey exploits his rivalry with Samuel Taylor Coleridge to structure many of the key features of his most famous work, *Confessions of an English Opium-Eater*. De Quincey's idolization of Coleridge began early and survived the anger and disappointment he felt after the collapse of their friendship and his discovery of Coleridge's intellectual duplicity. In *Confessions*, De Quincey's accounts of himself as a scholar of Greek literature, Ricardian economics, and Kantian philosophy are all galvanized by his knowledge that Coleridge too has worked in these areas. As opium addicts, De Quincey's experience of the drug overlaps with Coleridge's in a number of ways, while De Quincey differs from Coleridge—at least on the surface—in his claims about both the moral implications of drugged euphoria and the resolve needed to defeat addiction.③

Markus Poetzsch, in "Fearful Spaces: Thomas De Quincey's Sino-Anginophobia", gives an review on essayist Thomas De Quincey. This article points out that Thomas De Quincey mentions his Orientalist rhetoric as well as divided modes of writing, which is argued by scholar John Barrell who determined as identification and repudiation. An overview of the book *The Narcissism of Empire: Loss, Rage and Revenge in Thomas De Quincey, Robert Louis Stevenson, Arthur Conan Doyle, Rudyard Kipling and Isak Dinesen* by Diane Simmons is also presented.④

Daniel O'Quinn, in "Who Owns What: Slavery, Property, and Eschatological Compensation in Thomas De Quincey's Opium Writings", explores what it means to be a thing at a particularly

---

① Morrison R. "De Quincey and the Opium-Eater's Other Selves". Romanticism, 1999, 5(1): 87–103.
② Oakley W. "Physical Encounters as a Point of Contact between Sterne's *Journey* and De Quincey's *Confessions*". Romanticism, 2012, 18(2): 182–190.
③ Morrison R. "'Two faces, each of a confused countenance': Coleridge, De Quincey, and Contests of Authority". Romanticism, 2021, 27(3): 322–334.
④ Poetzsch M. "Fearful Spaces: Thomas De Quincey's Sino-Anginophobia". English Studies in Canada, 2015, 41(2/3): 27–41.

volatile moment when the consolidation of the European national subject and the racialization of colonized peoples were woven into the same historical process. The author of this article looks at ways in which Thomas De Quincey's writings have become exemplary for discussions of imperialism and colonialism from the 1770s to the mid-19th century. Topics discussed include weaving of the consolidation of the European national subject and the racialization of colonized peoples, and connection between De Quincey's analysis of the experience of opium and the problem of slavery.[1]

Philip Shaw, in "*On War*: De Quincey's Martial Sublime", discusses the article *On War* by Thomas De Quincey, published in the periodical *Macphail's Edinburgh Ecclesiastical Journal and Literary Review* in February 1848 and in revised form in the periodical *Selections, Grave and Gay* in 1854. It comments on De Quincey's conception of war as sublime. The author considers the relationship between war and Romantic discourse and the relationship of De Quincey's writings to the 1816 poem *Thanksgiving Ode* by William Wordsworth.[2]

Sue Chaplin, in "De Quincey's Gothic Innovations: *The Avenger*, 1838", presents a literary criticism of the book *The Avenger* by Thomas De Quincey. It outlines the novel's story of the persecution of a Jewish family in eastern Europe. The author argues that the novel is a prescient Gothic fiction that discusses the relationship between ethics and the law. The author also argues that the text of the book engages in what was an emerging human rights discourse.[3]

Ankhi Mukherjee, in "To Write like a Dream: Nineteenth-Century Legacies", examines works of literature that present themselves as psychological curiosities by using dreaming as a modality of displaced, unintentional, or even reluctant authorship. "What is it to write in, of, or like a dream? Who has the right to dream and who, conversely, is burdened with the nightmare of history? Themes to be considered include: dreamcomposition and the composition of dreams; narrative vs. lyrical form; the mediation of colonial commodities, like opium or travelogues, as what Nigel Leask calls; psychotropic technology; artistic autonomy vs. discursive formations of and cultural influences on dream mentation; the yoking of opposites and extremes in the compacted economy of the dream". The literary and critical works discussed are Samuel Taylor Coleridge's *Kubla Khan*, Thomas De Quincey's *Confessions of an English Opium-Eater*, Charles Dickens's *An Italian Dream*, Charles Kingsley's *Alton Locke*, and Sigmund Freud's *The Interpretation of Dreams*.[4]

---

[1] O'Quinn D. "Who Owns What: Slavery, Property, and Eschatological Compensation in Thomas De Quincey's Opium Writings". Texas Studies in Literature and Language, 2003, 45(3): 262-292.
[2] Shaw P. "*On War*: De Quincey's Martial Sublime". Romanticism. 2013, 19(1): 19-30.
[3] Chaplin S. "De Quincey's Gothic Innovations: *The Avenger*, 1838". Romanticism, 2011,17(3): 319-326.
[4] Mukherjee A. "To Write like a Dream: Nineteenth-Century Legacies". Criticism, 2019, 61(4): 509-526.

4. Translation Study

Brecht de Groote, in "On Not Being an Author: De Quincey's *Confessions* and the Performance of Romantic Translatorship", presents that through his *Confessions of an English Opium-Eater*, Thomas De Quincey effects a meticulously crafted entrance onto the literary scene: less a series of confidential notes than a stage-managed performance, the *Confessions of an English Opium-Eater* serves as a stage on which he announces his literary ambitions. One such set of performative acts has received little attention: it pertains less to establishing a ground from which to authoritatively create, than it does to laying down a structure through which to mediate. Acting on recent developments within literary criticism and translation studies, this article examines the ways in which the *Confessions of an English Opium-Eater* launches their writer on a career in interlingual and intercultural transfer, and how this performance of minority is designed to operate alongside other Romantic writers. The article ponders the successes and failures of mediation on display in emblematic scenes, and attends to how these chart the uneasy relationship between authorship and translatorship.[①]

5. Thematic Study

Cian Duffy, in "'My purpose was humbler, but also higher': Thomas De Quincey's *System of the Heavens*, Popular Science, and the Sublime", presents a literary criticism of the essay *System of the Heavens as Revealed by Lord Rosse's Telescopes*, by Thomas De Quincey. Particular focus is given to the essay's theme of astronomy, including in regard to the writer John Pringle Nichol's popularization of astronomy. The essay's depiction of the Orion Nebula, including the telescopic observations of it by astronomer William Edward Parsons (who is also referred to as the third Earl of Rosse and Lord Rosse), is discussed.[②]

Li-Hsin Hsu, in "The Romance of Transportation in Wordsworth, Emerson, De Quincey, and Dickinson", investigates diverging transatlantic attitudes towards mechanisation in the mid-nineteenth century by looking at the portrayals of steam engines in Anglo-American Romantic literary works by Wordsworth, Emerson, De Quincey and Dickinson. "Wolfgang Schivelbusch notes how time and space are 'annihilated' with the speed of industrialization. Walter Benjamin,

---

① De Groote B. "On Not Being an Author: De Quincey's *Confessions* and the Performance of Romantic Translatorship". Romanticism, 2021, 27(3): 262-271.

② Duffy C. "'My purpose was humbler, but also higher': Thomas De Quincey's *System of the Heavens*, Popular Science, and the Sublime". Romanticism, 2014, 20(1): 1-14.

alternatively, indicates how the metaphoric dressing up of steam engines as living creatures was a retreat from industrialization and modernization. Those conflicting perceptions of what David Nye calls the 'technological sublime' became sources of joy as well as sorrow for these authors. The essay examines how the literary representations of transportation show various literary attempts to make sense of and rewrite the technological promise of the future into distinct aesthetic experiences of modernity. Their imaginative engagement with the railway showcases a genealogy of metaphorical as well as mechanic transportation that indicates an evolving process of Romantic thought across the Atlantic Ocean". [1]

Annette Federico, in "The Violent Deaths of Oliver Twist", presents a literary criticism of the novel *Oliver Twist* by Charles Dickens. The author analyzes images of death in the novel and suggests that the novel represents a turning point on Dickens' writing career, after which he focused on themes of violence, death, and social reform. Specific topics discussed include death in Romantic literature by authors such as Thomas De Quincey and the murder of the character Nancy in *Oliver Twist*.[2]

Chris Pierson, in "The Reluctant Pirate: Godwin, Justice, and Property", presents a literary criticism of two editions of the book *Enquiry concerning Political Justice and Its Influence on Morals and Happiness* by William Godwin. It focuses on the relationship between private property and political justice through an exploration of themes such as public welfare, moral duties, and government responsibility. It provides critical analysis of Godwin's principles by the author Thomas De Quincey and speculates as to why Godwin altered his thoughts on property rights in different versions of the text.[3]

Robert S. Leventhal, in "The Rhetoric of Anarcho-Nihilistic Murder: Thomas Bernhard's *Das Kalkwerk*", examines the rhetoric of anarcho-nihilistic murder as highlighted in the book *Das Kalkwerk*, by Thomas Bernhard. The human being ultimately transforms all of nature into a model in its own image as inventor of images, analogies and metaphors. The model of modern subjectivity as a destructive power should reemerge in contemporary literature and literary theory in a volatile and problematical form. The first historical instance of a literal and amoral consideration of murder can be found in the early nineteenth century in the essay *On Murder Considered as One of the Fine Arts*, by Thomas De Quincey.[4]

---

[1] Hsu L-H. "The Romance of Transportation in Wordsworth, Emerson, De Quincey, and Dickinson". Romanticism, 2019, 25(1): 45-57.
[2] Federico A. "The Violent Deaths of Oliver Twist". Papers on Language and Literature, 2011, 47(4): 363-385.
[3] Pierson C. "The Reluctant Pirate: Godwin, Justice, and Property". Journal of the History of Ideas, 2010, 71(4): 569-591.
[4] Leventhal R S. "The Rhetoric of Anarcho-Nihilistic Murder: Thomas Bernhard's *Das Kalkwerk*". Modern Austrian Literature,1988, 21(3/4): 19-38.

6. Historical Study

Daniel Sanjiv Roberts, in "The Janus-face of Romantic Modernity: Thomas De Quincey's Metropolitan Imagination", discusses the urbanity and pastoral writing of 19th century British author Thomas De Quincey. It examines De Quincey's writing as compared to other Romantic-era poets and authors, as well as De Quincey's place among a genre some scholars have labeled Romantic metropolitanism. The essay discusses De Quincey's interest in London, England, and how the city influenced his writing, as well as De Quincey's evangelical upbringing.[①]

John Whale, in "De Quincey, Landscape, and Spiritual History", discusses that "De Quincey's writings contain 'reveries' that extend a Wordsworthian response to landscape and combine a sense of the infinite with a recognition of earthly labours. In the context of his troubled orientalism—in his articles *Ceylon*, *The Kalmuck Tartars*, and *Russia in 1812*, for example—his representation of landscape reveals a disturbed mixture of history and Christianity. His militant vision of civilisation secured by the apocalyptic battle of Waterloo is questioned by his construction of 'Eastern' Others and his powerful recognition of mortality". This pervasive sense of doubt also haunts the vision of England he put forward in *The English Mail-Coach*.[②]

7. Post-colonial Study

Peter J. Kitson, in "The Strange Case of Dr. White and Mr. De Quincey: Manchester, Medicine and Romantic Theories of Biological Racism", discusses an encounter between 19th century British essayist Thomas De Quincey and British surgeon Charles White. The article discusses De Quincey's collection of essays *Autobiographic Sketches* and the death of his sister, which White investigated along with British doctor Thomas Percival in Manchester, England, in 1791. The essay describes De Quincey's impressions of White as expressed in De Quincey's writing.[③]

David Higgins, in "Imagining the Exotic: De Quincey and Lamb in *The London Magazine*", discusses the contributions of British authors Charles Lamb and Thomas De Quincey to *The London Magazine* in the 1820s. The article focuses upon the October 1821 issue of *The London*

---

① Roberts D S. "The Janus-face of Romantic Modernity: Thomas De Quincey's Metropolitan Imagination". Romanticism, 2011, 17(3): 299-308.

② Whale J. "De Quincey, Landscape, and Spiritual History". Worldviews: Global Religions, Culture and Ecology, 2001, 5 (1): 4-19.

③ Kitson P J. "The Strange Case of Dr. White and Mr. De Quincey: Manchester, Medicine and Romantic Theories of Biological Racism". Romanticism, 2011, 17(3): 278-287.

Magazine, in which both Lamb and De Quincey published articles about exotic consumption and imagination. It examines Lamb's and De Quincey's writing on the exotic aspects of foreign culture. The article discusses Lamb's experiences as a clerk with the East India Company and its influence on his writing and his thoughts on British imperialism.[1]

8. Feminism Study

Julian North, in "De Quincey and the Inferiority of Women", examines letters written by De Quincey's daughters. The author of this article states that De Quincey's daughters were defenders of women's rights. The author also suggests that De Quincey's daughters criticized him for his views regarding the superiority of men over women. According to the author, the letters were written to book reviewer Francis Jacox.[2]

9. Comparative Literature Study

Joel D. Black, in "Levana: Levitation in Jean Paul and Thomas De Quincey", examines the treatment of Roman goddess Levana in the works of Jean Paul and Thomas De Quincey. Topics discussed include explanation of the emergence of Levana in Romantic literature; levitating functions performed by the figure of Levana in Jean Paul's writing *Levana oder Erziehlehre*; and description of De Quincey's figure of Levana.[3]

Eric Lindstrom, in "'Dog Sleep': Creaturely Exposure in De Quincey and Wordsworth", presents a critique of the book *Confessions of an English Opium-Eater* by Thomas De Quincey and the poem *The Prelude* by William Wordsworth, focusing on comparisons between each authors' romanticism and depiction of dogs and sleep. Themes of identity, references to the poet Samuel Coleridge, and the philosopher Jacques Derrida are also mentioned.[4]

John Ferguson, in "A Sea Change: Thomas De Quincey and Mr. Carmichael in *To the Lighthouse*", traces the origins of Augustus Carmichael, one of author Virginia Woolf's enigmatic characters and poet of *To the Lighthouse*, to Woolf's reading of Thomas De Quincey and to her complex attitude towards depression, life and friction. Topics discussed include characteristics of Carmichael; relation between De Quincey's stylistic approach and Carmichael's personality; and importance of the work for Woolf.[5]

---

[1] Higgins D. "Imagining the Exotic: De Quincey and Lamb in *The London Magazine*". Romanticism, 2011,17(3): 288–298.

[2] North J. "De Quincey and the Inferiority of Women". Romanticism, 2011, 17(3): 327–339.

[3] Black J D. "Levana: Levitation in Jean Paul and Thomas De Quincey". Comparative Literature, 1980, 32(1): 42–62.

[4] Lindstrom E. "'Dog Sleep': Creaturely Exposure in De Quincey and Wordsworth". Criticism, 2013, 55(3): 391–422.

[5] Ferguson J. "A Sea Change: Thomas De Quincey and Mr. Carmichael in *To the Lighthouse*". Journal of Modern Literature, 1987, 14(1): 45–63.

Chapter 8
Bertrand Russell

Bertrand Russell (1872-1970)

  Bertrand Russell was a British philosopher, logician, and social reformer, a founding figure in the analytic movement in Anglo-American philosophy, and recipient of the Nobel Prize for Literature in 1950. Russell's contributions to logic, epistemology, and the philosophy of mathematics established him as one of the foremost philosophers of the 20th century. To the general public, however, he was best known as a campaigner for peace and as a popular writer on social, political, and moral subjects. During a long, productive, and often turbulent life, he published more than 70 books and about 2,000 articles, married four times, became involved in innumerable public controversies, and was honoured and reviled in almost equal measure throughout the world. Russell's article on the philosophical consequences of relativity appeared in the 13th edition of the *Encyclopedia Britannica*.[①]

[①] https://www.britannica.com/biography/Bertrand-Russell.

Critical Perspectives

1. Narrative Study

Mathew Mercuri, in "Publishing Your Work: An Editor's Perspective", discusses some of the lessons he learned during his time as editor of *Journal of Evaluation in Clinical Practice*. Topics mentioned include rejection of manuscripts due to failure to understand or follow the Author Guidelines, the impact of how the material within the manuscript is organized on how it will be received by the reviewer, and an essay by British philosopher Bertrand Russell on how to communicate effectively in academic contexts.[1]

Justin D. Barnard, in "Brains but No Blood: C. S. Lewis' Obsession with Naturalism", discusses the element of philosophical belief "naturalism" in literary works of the author C. S. Lewis. Topics discussed include Lewis's poetry book *Spirits in Bondage: A Cycle of Lyrics*, Bertrand Russell's essay *A Free Man's Worship*, and Lewis's argument against naturalism and his beliefs on Christian Apologetics faith.[2]

2. Philosophical Study

William H. Brenner, in "Natural Law, Motives, and Freedom of the Will", focuses on a Wittgensteinian view on natural law, motives and freedom of the will. Topics discussed include natural law and compulsion; definition of unconscious motivation; and an excerpt of an essay by Bertrand Russell on compulsion.[3]

---

[1] Mercuri M. "Publishing Your Work: An Editor's Perspective". Journal of Evaluation in Clinical Practice, 2020, 26(1): 3-6.

[2] Barnard J D. "Brains but No Blood: C. S. Lewis' Obsession with Naturalism". Renewing Minds: A Journal of Christian Thought, 2013(4): 27-35.

[3] Brenner W H. "Natural Law, Motives, and Freedom of the Will". Philosophical Investigations, 2001, 24(3): 246-261.

Chapter 9
Virginia Woolf

Virginia Woolf (1882-1941)

Virginia Woolf was an English writer, and one of the foremost modernists of the twentieth century. During the interwar period, Woolf was a significant figure in London literary society and a central figure in the influential Bloomsbury Group of intellectuals. Her most famous works include the novels *Mrs. Dalloway* (1925), *To the Lighthouse* (1927) and *Orlando* (1928), and the book-length essay *A Room of One's Own* (1929), with its famous dictum, "A woman must have money and a room of her own if she is to write fiction". Woolf suffered from severe bouts of mental illness throughout her life, thought to have been the result of what is now termed bipolar disorder, and committed suicide by drowning in 1941 at the age of 59.[1]

---

[1] https://www.columbia.edu/~ajl2217/wikipedia/.

Critical Perspectives

1. Biographical Study

Roxanne Covelo, in "Thomas De Quincey in the Essays of Virginia Woolf: 'Prose Poetry' and the Autobiographic Mode", argues that "British author Thomas De Quincey makes brief but frequent appearances in Woolf's essays of literary criticism, in which she examines what she understands to be their shared aesthetic objectives in the areas of prose-style and (auto) biographic writing. Interestingly, although Woolf often frames these objectives in terms that may be called post- or even anti-Victorian, her approach to De Quincey's work is strongly mediated by the critical scholarship of her father, the Victorian critic and biographer Leslie Stephen, and his own essays on De Quincey published between 1869 and 1927".[1]

David Nasaw, in "Historians and Biography: Introduction", discusses various reports published within the issue on historians and biography, including one by Liana Vardi on the fashion for scholarly historical biography, and one by Alice Kessler-Harris on Virginia Woolf's essay *The Art of Biography*.[2]

2. Feminism Study

Margarita E. Sánchez Cuervo, in "The Appeal to Audience through Figures of Thought in Virginia Woolf's Feminist Essays", discusses the presence of figures of thought in some well-known feminist essays by Virginia Woolf, regarding feminist concerns including the women in culture and society as well as their success. It notes that the thoughts of Woolf are expressed in prose with arguments and rhetorical figures. Explored are financial desires of women, along with social constraints imposed on them. Woolf tries to make readers aware of her feminist views by using expressive resources like figures of speech or schemes, tropes and figures of thought in her writing. Figures of thought can be defined as those specific gestures which are designed to interact with the audience. Their use is connected with the functional use of language in the

---

[1] Covelo R. "Thomas De Quincey in the Essays of Virginia Woolf: 'Prose Poetry' and the Autobiographic Mode". Journal of Modern Literature, 2018, 41(4): 31-47.

[2] Nasaw D. "Historians and Biography: Introduction". The American Historical Review, 2009, 114(3): 573-578.

sense that they may draw readers' attention away from the textual content and toward the context. The figures analyzed are enallage of person, erotema, ecphonesis, prosopopeia, aposiopesis and prolepsis.①

Linda O'Neill, in "Embodied Hermeneutics: Gadamer Meets Woolf in *A Room of One's Own*", points out that Hans-Georg Gadamer has been criticized by a wide range of feminist scholars who argue that his work neglects feminine aspects of understanding, many of which are essential to sound theorizing about educational contexts. In this essay, Linda O'Neill employs Virginia Woolf's classic gender analysis both as a foil for Gadamer's philosophical hermeneutics and as an exemplar of feminist reasoning. Through her striking descriptions of embodied tradition, language, and transcendence, Woolf challenges and enriches Gadamer's work. Bringing Gadamer into conversation with Woolf offers expanded horizons for philosophers of education who choose to ground their studies of teachers and learners in a feminist epistemology resonant with the rich ambiguity of educational experience. This comparison, O'Neill concludes, suggests that the pluralistic reasoning of feminist inquiry offers engendered, embodied insights absent from Gadamer's hermeneutics and crucial to what Patti Lather calls "fieldwork in philosophy", an investigative alternative capable of informing sustainable educational policy, practice, and reform.②

Victoria L. Smith, in "'Ransacking the Language': Finding the Missing Goods in Virginia Woolf's *Orlando*", contends that Virginia Woolf's peculiar and fantastical "biography" of Vita Sackville-West effects a double compensation, situating *Orlando* within a matrix of biographical, cultural, and literary concerns. "By attending to the tensions between the real and the fictional/fantastic and the public and private, I suggest that the text restores lost loves and lost objects to both Vita Sackville-West and Virginia Woolf. The other compensation the novel effects is located at the level of representation". *Orlando* is a complex interplay between Woolf and Sackville-West. It is also Woolf's own story of the inadequacy of language to name the "thing itself" and to represent women, a story that nevertheless self-consciously conveys through language the very things she suggests language is incapable of.③

3. Narrative Study

Matthew Weber, in "Those Dots: Suspension and Interruption in Virginia Woolf's *Three*

---

① Sánchez Cuervo M E. "The Appeal to Audience through Figures of Thought in Virginia Woolf's Feminist Essays". Renascence, 2016, 68(2): 127-143.

② O'Neill L. "Embodied Hermeneutics: Gadamer Meets Woolf in *A Room of One's Own*". Educational Theory, 2007, 57(3): 325-337.

③ Smith V L. "'Ransacking the Language': Finding the Missing Goods in Virginia Woolf's *Orlando*". Journal of Modern Literature, 2006, 29(4): 57-75.

Guineas and *Between the Acts*", argues that "Virginia Woolf's essay *Three Guineas*(1938) and her last novel *Between the Acts*(1941) refuse easy recuperation by progressive and activist politics. Emphasis on redemptive aspects of those texts elides the characteristic suspension and interruption of progress in Woolf's late works. The suspension is most strikingly evoked by Woolf's interruptive 'dots'. The dots intervene at pivotal moments in *Three Guineas*, halting the progress of the essay and suspending its readers between a desire for progressive action and a desire for withdrawal from action. Similarly disruptive of affirmative conclusions (and riddled with dots), *Between the Acts* dramatizes a yearning for stable collectivities that might exist outside of the apparently inevitable violence of war. But the novel suspends its own utopian project".[①]

Emma Sutton, in "'Putting Words on the Backs of Rhythm': Woolf, *Street Music*, and *The Voyage Out*", explores Virginia Woolf's representation of rhythm in two early texts—her neglected 1905 essay *Street Music* and her first novel, *The Voyage Out* (1915). It teases out the texts' characterizations of musical, literary, bodily and urban rhythms, considering their implications for a theory of literary rhythm more broadly. Arguing that rhythm has a central place in Woolf's writing practice, prose style and theories of writing, the essay charts the relationship between rhythm, individuality and literary value in these texts, and in selected correspondence, diary extracts, essays and fiction.[②]

Anca Mihaela Dobrinescu, in "Modernist/ Postmodernist Considerations on the Margin-Centre Interplay", focuses on the margin-centre interplay as approached by modernism and postmodernism and aims at demonstrating that the relationship between the margin and the centre, unquestionably central to the discourse of postmodernism, was of equal interest to the modernist writers in spite of their apparent indifference to their immediate cultural environment. "By analysing Virginia Woolf's book-length essay *Three Guineas* and Salman Rushdie's *Step across This Line*, we intend to prove that both modernism and postmodernism are sensitive to issues related to cultural identity, proposing relatively similar solutions to the crisis of intercultural communication characteristic of the modern world".[③]

Thomas Reinert, in "Joan Didion and Political Irony", argues that there is a tradition for the political irony that comes from a literary renunciation of the literary, as used by Joan Didion. Topics discussed include John Ruskin's essay on fallacy; essay by Virginia Woolf; and Didion's essay *The White Album*.[④]

---

① Weber M. "Those Dots: Suspension and Interruption in Virginia Woolf's *Three Guineas* and *Between the Acts*". Journal of Modern Literature, 2017, 40(3): 18–34.
② Sutton E. "'Putting Words on the Backs of Rhythm': Woolf, *Street Music*, and *The Voyage Out*". Paragraph, 2010, 33(2): 176–196.
③ Dobrinescu A M. "Modernist/ Postmodernist Considerations on the Margin-Centre Interplay". Petroleum – Gas University of Ploiesti Bulletin, Philology Series, 2009, 61(2): 45–50.
④ Reinert T. "Joan Didion and political irony". Raritan, 1996, 15(3):122–136.

4. Psychoanalysis Study

Michael Lucey, in "Voice to Voice: Self-Affirmation in *The Years*", examines the complex questions posed by Virginia Woolf in her late essay *Anon* and her poem *The Years*. Topics discussed include whether it is possible to cite a bird; the possibility to engage in conversation with an animal in a way that is self-affirming; and excerpts from both works.[1]

---

[1] Lucey M. "Voice to Voice: Self-affirmation in *The Years*". Novel: A Forum on Fiction, 1991, 24(3): 257-281.

Chapter 10
George Orwell

George Orwell (1903-1950)

George Orwell was an English novelist, essayist, and critic famous for his novels *Animal Farm* (1945) and *Nineteen Eighty-four* (1949), the latter a profound anti-utopian novel that examines the dangers of totalitarian rule. Born Eric Arthur Blair, Orwell never entirely abandoned his original name, but his first book, *Down and Out in Paris and London*, appeared in 1933 as the work of George Orwell (the surname he derived from the beautiful River Orwell in East Anglia). In time his nom de plume became so closely attached to him that few people but relatives knew his real name was Blair. The change in name corresponded to a profound shift in Orwell's lifestyle, in which he changed from a pillar of the British imperial establishment into a literary and political rebel.[1]

---

[1] https://www.britannica.com/biography/George-Orwell.

Critical Perspectives

1. Narrative Study

Douglas E. Abrams, in "George Orwell's Classic Essay on Writing: The Best Style 'Handbook' for Lawyers and Judges (Part Ⅰ)", discusses the reported importance of author George Orwell's 1946 essay on writing entitled "Politics and the English Language", focusing on the views of Judge Richard A. Posner and Nobel Prize-winning economist Paul Krugman regarding Orwell's essay. The late U.S. Supreme Court Justice Felix Frankfurter is mentioned, along with writing style-related information for American lawyers and judges. Metaphors and figures of speech are examined, along with various American legal cases.[①]

2. Linguistics Study

Nellufar Yeasmin, Abul Kalam Azad, and Jannatul Ferdoush, in "*Shooting an Elephant*: A Stylistic Analysis", present that "Stylistic analysis has always been an important aid in understanding literary texts. Stylistic knowledge enriches readers' understanding of literary pieces and can supplement their knowledge of literary interpretation. With this view in mind, literary texts have been analyzed from linguistic point of view. The present study looks at an important political essay *Shooting an Elephant* by George Orwell. The text has attracted wide recognition and appreciation from the literary critics. It portrays Orwell's anti-imperialistic view which is presented through an incident, the shooting of an elephant. The theme is presented in a fantastic way and this is evident from Orwell's use of lexis, syntax, cohesive ties, point of view, and figures of speech. A closer look at the linguistic devices indicates that his style matches his objectives and that he has been successful in attaining his political, artistic as well as thematic aims through his elegant style".[②]

Laurie Endicott Thomas, in "Passive Voice and Expletive Constructions", offers

---

[①] Abrams D E. "George Orwell's Classic Essay on Writing: The Best Style 'Handbook' for Lawyers and Judges(Part Ⅰ)". Tennessee Bar Journal, 2014, 50(5): 20–26.

[②] Yeasmin N, Azad A K, Ferdoush J. "*Shooting an Elephant*: A Stylistic Analysis". ASA University Review, 2013, 7(1): 27–36.

information on using the passive voice or expletive constructions in George Orwell's writing. The author of this essay takes a careful study of novelist George Orwell's essay *Politics and the English Language*, and states that the book *The Elements of Style* by E. B. White and William Strunk asks writers to avoid using the passive voice.[①]

3. Biographical Study

James Stillwaggon, in "Inviolable Laws, Impossible to Keep: Orwell on Education, Suffering, and the Loss of Childhood", presents that "Scholars from multiple disciplines have commented on the divided nature of childhood as a historical construction: a period of life to be valued in itself as well as a means to adulthood". In this essay, the author considers George Orwell's *Such, Such Were the Joys*, an autobiographical account of his childhood education, as a site of conflicting views on childhood. On analyzing Orwell's own conflicted memories, Stillwaggon describes education as a process of suffering the loss of childhood and inquires into the adult subject's maintenance of such loss in memory. Drawing from Deborah Britzman and Jacques Lacan, Stillwaggon suggests that the adult subject's maintenance of a childhood state irrevocably lost is a melancholic identification against the transformative powers of the school.[②]

Stephen Miller, in "Orwell Once More", presents literary criticism which profiles English writer George Orwell. His essays are often found in freshman college readers and in anthologies of English writers, and two of his novels—*Animal Farm* and *Nineteen Eighty-four*—have been translated into many languages. Why biographers are interested in Orwell is understandable because he led a life that was unusual for a writer. He was a British policeman in Burma, a dishwasher in Paris, and an investigative journalist in England; he was also a bookstore assistant, schoolmaster, grocer, and foreign correspondent. Orwell's interest in military affairs is apparent in his essays and reviews, many of which touch on military questions.[③]

4. Special Study

James Tyner, in "Landscape and the Mask of Self in George Orwell's *Shooting an Elephant*", argues that "Recent work in geography has focused attention on the imbrication of landscape and literature. A dominant thread of these 'fictive geographies' has been a concern

---

① Thomas L E. "Passive Voice and Expletive Constructions". American Medical Writers Association Journal, 2015, 30(4): 188-189.
② Stillwaggon J. "Inviolable Laws, Impossible to Keep: Orwell on Education, Suffering, and the Loss of Childhood". Educational Theory, 2010, 60(1): 61-80.
③ Miller S. "Orwell Once More". The Sewanee Review, 2004, 112(4): 595-618.

with how imagined landscapes contribute to the constitution of self. Informed especially by post-structuralism and post-colonialism, geographers have recently provided critical readings of novels, short stories and essays. In this paper, I provide a reading of George Orwell's essay *Shooting an Elephant*. The writings of Orwell reveal a long-standing engagement with issues of humanity and subjectivity, and I contend that this essay, rather than a straightforward polemic against British imperialism, reveals a concern primarily with the constitution of self within a colonial landscape. Orwell's essay thus provides insight into the processes whereby human subjectivities interact with space and structures".①

5. Historical Study

Peter Schwendener, in "Reflections of a Bookstore Type", presents the reflections on George Orwell's experience as a bookseller. Topics discussed include reference to George Orwell's essay about bookshops and booksellers; problems in bookselling; taboos in bookselling; differing habits of men and women book buyers; and turnover rate of employees.②

John King, in "Flying the Flag", discusses the reasons behind the embarrassments among the left about patriotism, focusing on the policies of Jeremy Corbyn as the leader of the British Labour Party. Topics mentioned include the wider belief that the Labour is somewhat anti-British, author George Orwell who wrote the classic essay *The Lion & the Unicorn: Socialism and the English Genius*, and the Scottish National Party (SNP).③

Debbie Millman, in "The Text Issue", presents an introduction which cites the inscription of text as the theme of the current issue and discusses topics including text messaging, the social and personal dimensions of reading and writing, and an essay by English author George Orwell classifying the purposes for which people write.④

Bruce Reed, in "Life after 7/7", expresses views on the bombings in the public transportation system in London, England on July 7, 2005. Topics discussed include significance of philosopher George Orwell's essay about British war and politics to the bombing; comments on the approach used by U. S. President George W. Bush in the September 11 Attack; and criticism of Labourite George Galloway against British Prime Minister Tony Blair on the country's security services.⑤

---

① Tyner J. "Landscape and the Mask of Self in George Orwell's *Shooting an Elephant*". Area, 2005, 37(3): 260-267.
② Schwendener P. "Reflections of a Bookstore Type". The American Scholar,1995, 64(4): 607-608.
③ King J. "Flying the Flag". New Statesman, 2016, 145(5298): 28-29.
④ Millman D. "The Text Issue". Print, 2015, 69(4): 41.
⑤ Reed B. "Life after 7/7". Blueprint, 2005, 2005(3): 13.

6. Ethical Study

Danny Heitman, in "Wendell Berry in the Library of America", offers information on American novelist Wendell Berry and his book *What I Stand for Is What I Stand on*. Topics discussed include the National Humanities Medal received by him in 2010; Wendell Berry's concern with the subtle corruptions of language, which bring about political and spiritual corruption, too; and the declarations of a moralist in his essays like novelist George Orwell.[①]

7. Psychoanalysis Study

William Germano, in "Why We Write", discusses the factors that prompt a person to write fictitious books. In his 1946 essay *Why I Write*, George Orwell describes the writing of books by making up stories and holding conversations with imaginary persons as a possible symptom of psychological disorder. Orwell settles on four great motives for writing. These motives are sheer egoism, aesthetic enthusiasm, historical impulse and political purpose. These four factors drove Eric Blair's prose. Academic writes if it is only a necessity of the education industry, no wonder one's fingers get tired. No human activity can sap the strength from body and life from spirit as much as writing in which one doesn't believe.[②]

[①] Heitman D. "Wendell Berry in the Library of America". Humanities, 2019, 40(4): 13.
[②] Germano W. "Why We Write". The Chronicle of Higher Education, 2006, 52(40): 5.

Chapter 11
John Boynton Priestley

John Boynton Priestley(1894-1984)

John Boynton Priestley was a British novelist, playwright, and essayist, noted for his varied output and his ability for shrewd characterization. Priestley served in the infantry in World War Ⅰ and then studied English literature at Trinity College, Cambridge. He thereafter worked as a journalist and first established a reputation with the essays collected in *The English Comic Characters* (1925). He achieved enormous popular success with *The Good Companions* (1929), a picaresque novel about a group of traveling performers. This was followed in 1930 by his most solidly crafted novel, *Angel Pavement*, a sombre, realistic depiction of the lives of a group of office workers in London. His other more important novels are *Bright Day* (1946) and *Lost Empires* (1965).

Critical Perspectives

1. Narrative Study

Simon Rycroft, and Roger Jenness, in "J. B. Priestley: Bradford and a Provincial Narrative of England, 1913-1933", discuss that "J. B. Priestley's writing has been used to explore aspects of landscape and Englishness. Through an analysis of Priestley's early journalism in *Bradford Pioneer* and *The Yorkshire Observer*, we argue that his critical disengagement to most of the landscapes of England was based on a connection to the landscapes of his youth in Bradford where he first developed his fictional and documentary narrative style. In his early journalism, Priestley articulated a sense of dwelling in Bradford that was rooted in the experience of two distinct local landscapes: the spaces of the city and the nature of the surrounding upland and moorland. Priestley's geographical ideal balanced the civility of the Edwardian city embedded in a landscape that offered escape to and commune with nature. The existential balance between the two was, we argue, central to the narrative geographies developed by Priestley in his fiction which is illustrated through an analysis of his two early novels: *The Good Companions* (1929) and *Angel Pavement* (1930). We suggest that the ways in which Priestley's interwar writing expressed dwelling in local landscapes might be thought of as a critical provincialisation of London and England".[1]

2. New Historicism Study

Michael John Law, in "Charabancs and Social Class in 1930s Britain", argues that "The renowned writer J. B. Priestley suggested in 1934 that the motor coach had annihilated the old distinction between rich and poor passengers in Britain. This article considers how true this was by examining the relationship between charabancs, motor coaches and class. It shows that this important vehicle of inter-war working class mobility had a complicated relationship with class, identifying three distinct forms of this method of travel. It positions the charabanc alongside historical responses to unwelcome steamer and railway day-trippers, and examines how resorts

---

[1] Rycroft S, Jenness R. "J. B. Priestley: Bradford and a Provincial Narrative of England, 1913-1933". Social and Cultural Geography, 2012, 13(8): 957-976.

provided separate class-based entertainment for these holidaymakers. Using the case study of a new charabanc-welcoming pub, the Prospect Inn, it proposes that, in the late 1930s, some pubs were beginning to offer charabanc customers facilities that were almost the match of their middle class equivalent. Motor coaches and charabancs contributed to the process of social convergence in inter-war Britain".[1]

Martin Walter, in " 'In the Beginning There Was the Coal Pit': Discovering Industrial Landscapes in Interwar Britain and Weimar Germany in the Travel-writings of H. V. Morton, J. B. Priestley and Heinrich Hauser", argues that following the World War Ⅰ, "the travelogue as a literary genre, and the process of travelling as a performative act, functioned as vehicles for renegotiating ideas of space—a phenomenon that surfaced especially during encounters with and perceptions of industrial landscapes. Struggling between nostalgic notions of a pre-industrial countryside and the coming-to-terms with the new places of modernity, landscapes became not only narratively framed as contested spaces, but, moreover, discursive fields in which ideological struggles of belonging, progress and social order were fought out".[2]

---

[1] Law M J. "Charabancs and Social Class in 1930s Britain". The Journal of Transport History, 2015, 36(1): 41-57.
[2] Walter M. " 'In the Beginning There Was the Coal Pit': Discovering Industrial Landscapes in Interwar Britain and Weimar Germany in the Travel-writings of H. V. Morton, J. B. Priestley and Heinrich Hauser". National Identities, 2014, 16(3): 225-237.

Chapter 12
Benjamin Franklin

Benjamin Franklin (1706-1790)

  Benjamin Franklin had already made great contributions to American society before he became involved in the movement for Independence. His career as a printer, publisher, scientist, inventor, postmaster, politician and diplomat had made him famous around the world. As a diplomat with years of experience representing the colonies in Europe, his role during and after the conflict was essential in securing an independent and prosperous nation. Born in 1706, he was one of the oldest and most distinguished of the Founding Fathers. Along with John Adams, Franklin was chosen to advise Thomas Jefferson on the drafting of *The Declaration of Independence* in 1776. This team also journeyed to France together as part of a delegation to secure an alliance with France, Britain's perpetual nemesis. Later, Franklin and Adams would be part of the American delegation during the peace talks that led to the *Treaty of Paris*, ending the Revolutionary War on favorable terms. Despite all of his success, the humble Franklin still preferred to be known as a printer first and foremost.[1]

---

[1] https://www.benjaminfranklinbio.com/.

Critical Perspectives

1. Biographical Study

Shai Afsai, in "Benjamin Franklin's Influence on Mussar Thought and Practice: A Chronicle of Misapprehension", argues that Benjamin Franklin's ideas and writings may be said to have had an impact on Jewish thought and practice. This influence occurred posthumously, primarily through his autobiography and by way of Menachem Mendel Levin's *Cheshbon HaNefesh* ("The Book of Spiritual Accounting", 1808), which introduced Franklin's method for moral perfection to a Hebrew-reading Jewish audience. This historical development has confused Judaic scholars, and Franklin specialists have been largely oblivious to it. Remedying the record on this matter illustrates how even within the presumably insular world of Eastern European rabbinic Judaism—far from the deism of the trans-Atlantic Enlightenment—pre-Reform, pre-Conservative Jewish religion was affected by broader currents of thought.[①]

Jay Tolson, in "The Many Faces of Benjamin Franklin", discusses the role of Benjamin Franklin as a founding father for the U.S. colonies. Topics discussed include consideration of the historical images depicting Franklin as a newspaperman, essayist, pamphleteer, memoirist, and correspondent; his understanding of the relationships between the media and the public; criticism of Franklin by writers such as D. H. Lawrence and Sinclair Lewis; and influence of Franklin on the policies of the U.S. Constitution.[②]

Danielle Bobker, in "Intimate Points: The Dash in *The Autobiography of Benjamin Franklin*", presents criticism on the book *The Autobiography of Benjamin Franklin*, written by Benjamin Franklin. Particular focus is given to Franklin's use of dashes in his writing. Additional topics discussed include details relating to the narrative of the story, the history of the dash as a punctuation mark, and Franklin's writing style.[③]

James W. Marcum, in "Genius or Dynamic Learner? Benjamin Franklin's Path to Greatness", discusses that "While the remarkable accomplishments of Benjamin Franklin are

---

① Afsai S. "Benjamin Franklin's Influence on Mussar Thought and Practice: A Chronicle of Misapprehension". Review of Rabbinic Judaism, 2019, 22(2): 228-276.
② Tolson J. "The Many Faces of Benjamin Franklin". U.S. News & World Report, 2003, 134(22): 34-38.
③ Bobker D. "Intimate Points: The Dash in *The Autobiography of Benjamin Franklin*". Papers on Language and Literature, 2013, 49(4): 415-443.

unparalleled, the means of their attainment can be considered more accessible to ordinary people and not necessarily attributable to a special genius. The steady development of Franklin's knowledge and skills is traced in light of a new model of 'dynamic learning', which is a method that can be followed by many. The method involves reading, writing, collaboration, and active, hands-on experience. Simple steps are suggested for testing the method in the classroom". ①

2. Psychological Study

James J. Dillon, in "Benjamin Franklin: A Wonder-Based Approach to Life and Learning", focuses on the views of American journalist, printer and statesman Benjamin Franklin on education in the U.S. It mentions that Franklin's sense of wonder and curiosity to life and learning made him a model for children. It also believes that his wonder-based approach to life and learning enabled him to make discoveries and inventions. It also states that Franklin underwent self-education.②

Joseph Fichtelberg, in "The Complex Image: Text and Reader in *The Autobiography of Benjamin Franklin*", focuses on the depiction on attitude of Benjamin Franklin in his autobiography in the United States. Topics discussed include struggles on adapting private reminiscences; notes on youth experiences; and assessment on literary style.③

Joseph Chaves, in "Polite Mentors and Franklin's 'Exquisite Pleasure': Sociability, Prophylaxis, and Dependence in *The Autobiography*", presents a critical analysis of Benjamin Franklin's *The Autobiography*. "Hugh J. Dawson and Jay Fliegelman have described Franklin's elders, persuasively and influentially, as 'surrogate fathers', who provide paternal guidance and approbation on the model of the educative, affective family, modifying it by making it less hierarchical and intrusive". Fliegelman identifies *The Autobiography*'s anti-patriarchal critique with its function as an attack on the fixed orders of society and the government of names. "Fliegelman and Dawson insist that Franklin's eventual assertion of integrity and self-determination necessitates his abandoning these surrogates toward the end of part, because the relationships with elder mentors entail elements of dependence and artifice".④

Ada Van Gastel, in "Franklin and Freud: Love in *The Autobiography*", focuses on the impact of Benjamin Franklin's autobiography on civilization in the United States. Topics

---

① Marcum J W. "Genius or Dynamic Learner? Benjamin Franklin's Path to Greatness". The Social Studies, 2008, 99(3): 99-104.
② Dillon J J. "Benjamin Franklin: A Wonder-Based Approach to Life and Learning". Encounter, 2009, 22(4): 38-47.
③ Fichtelberg J. "The Complex Image: Text and Reader in *The Autobiography of Benjamin Franklin*". Early American Literature,1988, 23(2): 202-216.
④ Chaves J. "Polite Mentors and Franklin's 'Exquisite Pleasure': Sociability, Prophylaxis, and Dependence in *The Autobiography*". Early American Literature, 2007, 42(3): 555-571.

discussed include consideration as landmark in secularization and corruption of the colonial period, and examination on handling of feelings towards the opposite sex.[①]

3. New Historical Study

Matthew Smith, in "Franklin's Gambit", features Benjamin Franklin and his love of chess and diplomatic skills. Also cited are Franklin's deployment in Paris, France in 1777 to negotiate a U.S. alliance with France, his fellow revolutionaries who also loved chess like Thomas Jefferson, Israel Putnam, and James Madison, and his works on chess like his book *Autobiography* and his 1779 essay *The Morals of Chess*.[②]

John Steele Gordon, in "Fabulous Franklin", features Benjamin Franklin, one of the founding fathers of the U.S. Also cited are the other signatories of *The Declaration of Independence* or Constitution like George Washington, Thomas Jefferson, John Adams, and James Madison, Franklin's diplomatic efforts in France to convince the French to intervene in the American Revolution, and his major role in the intellectual movement called Enlightenment.[③]

Louis Sirico, in "Benjamin Franklin, Prayer, and the Constitutional Convention: History as Narrative", focuses on the important role played by former-President Benjamin Franklin in shaping the laws and cultural traditions in the U.S. It highlights Franklin's proposal to include in the Constitutional Convention the orders to open meetings with a prayer, which has been adopted in the popular and political history of the country. However, several narratives argue that several Convention members did not accept and implement Franklin's proposal.[④]

Michael Sletcher, in "Domesticity: The Human Side of Benjamin Franklin", profiles the great American statesman Benjamin Franklin and features his human side as written in his autobiography. The author highlights Franklin's marriage to his wife, Deborah Read Franklin. "As one of America's leading founding fathers, his popularity as a historical subject should not surprise us; he was, after all, a significant figure who embodied the values of not only the eighteenth century but America's future. Franklin, in other words, personified the ideals of free enterprise found in nineteenth and twentieth century America—the possibility of great achievement and worldly success through natural ability and hard work, or what we call 'the American dream'". Unlike the proverbial chartacters written in *Poor Richard's Almanack*, he was not the Franklin known for his thirteen virtues. However, Franklin had some share of

---

① Van Gastel A. "Franklin and Freud: Love in *The Autobiography*". Early American Literature, 1990, 25(2): 168-182.
② Smith M. "Franklin's Gambit". American History, 2022, 57(2): 24-31.
③ Gordon J S. "Fabulous Franklin". The New Criterion, 2021, 39(5): 23-27.
④ Sirico L. "Benjamin Franklin, Prayer, and the Constitutional Convention: History as Narrative". Legal Communication and Rhetoric, 2013(10): 89-124.

infidelities and sexual improprieties despite being married to Deborah. "Yet there is another—more human—side of this great revolutionary hero, which is equally interesting but less well known to the public: Franklin the husband and father". The author assesses the family life of Franklin.[①]

Alberto Lena, in "Benjamin Franklin's 'Canada Pamphlet' or 'The Ravings of a Mad Prophet': Nationalism, Ethnicity and Imperialism", points out that "Written in response to the political debate generated by the London press after the fail of Quebec in 1759, and establishing Benjamin Franklin's notion of American nationalism before the American Revolution, 'The Canada Pamphlet' stands as one of the most complex and sophisticated pieces of pre-revolutionary American thought. In it Franklin entertained the idea of an homogeneous American population in manners, language and religion as a reaction against ethnic and political warfare within Europe. Drawing on the ideas of Hobbes, Hume and Spinoza, Franklin believed that political and ethnic relations were exclusively dominated by power, leaving no room for multiculturalism in America, preferring instead the implementation of the British Crown model in the colonies to foster internal peace there". [②]

Karen M. Rosenthall, in "A Generative Populace: Benjamin Franklin's Economic Agendas", features Benjamin Franklin, one of the founding fathers of the U.S., as well as his economic agendas. Also cited are Franklin's book *The Autobiography of Benjamin Franklin* that made him a progenitor of unique political economy ideals, Franklin's move to advance both agrarian republicanism and commercialism, and his comment on British economic policy in relation to the economic potential in the U.S.[③]

Jennifer T. Kennedy, in "Death Effects: Revisting the Conceit of Franklin's *Memoir*", provides information on the book *Memoir*, by Benjamin Franklin, which deals with death and afterdeath. Topics discussed include brief information on the life and death of Franklin; details of reincarnation theory; and speculation on ghosts.[④]

Kevin J. Hayes, in "The Board of Trade's 'Cruel Sarcasm': A Neglected Franklin Source", discusses Benjamin Franklin's indignation with British attitudes toward America as illustrated by the Board of Trade's report on a Plantation Act intended to prevent the importation of convicts. Topics discussed include functions of the board; acts passed by Pennsylvania from

---

① Sletcher M. "Domesticity: The Human Side of Benjamin Franklin". OAH Magazine of History, 2006, 20(2): 47-52.
② Lena A. "Benjamin Franklin's 'Canada Pamphlet' or 'The Ravings of a Mad Prophet': Nationalism, Ethnicity and Imperialism". European Journal of American Culture, 2001, 20(1): 36-49.
③ Rosenthall K M. "A Generative Populace: Benjamin Franklin's Economic Agendas". Early American Literature, 2016, 51(3): 571-598.
④ Kennedy J T. "Death Effects: Revisting the Conceit of Franklin's *Memoir*". Early American Literature, 2001, 36(2): 201-234.

1722 to 1742/43 limiting convict transportation; and Franklin's first literary use of the board's "cruel sarcasm".①

4. Cultural Study

Martin H. Levinson, in "Benjamin Franklin: A Time-binder Extra Ordinaire", discusses the late scientist and civic leader Benjamin Franklin and his contribution to human knowledge across time. It notes that the aphorisms Franklin published in his yearly almanac helped define the nation's values as it emerged from its Puritan past. It notes Franklin's invention of the metal stove as an improvement over the inefficient fireplace, and of the lightning rod, neither of which he patented. Franklin's civic and diplomatic accomplishments are noted.②

5. Religious Study

Arthur A. Chiel, in "Benjamin Franklin, His Genesis Text", focuses on the views of Benjamin Franklin on the book *Genesis*. Topics discussed include imitation of Biblical text; attribution of parables to involvement in international affairs; and characterization of Abraham as an offering of hospitality in return of praising God.③

---

① Hayes K J. "The Board of Trade's 'Cruel Sarcasm': A Neglected Franklin Source". Early American Literature,1993, 28 (2): 171-176.
② Levinson M H. "Benjamin Franklin: A Time-binder Extra Ordinaire". ETC: A Review of General Semantics, 2009, 66(3): 269-277.
③ Chiel A A. "Benjamin Franklin, His Genesis Text". Judaism, 1976, 25(3): 353-356.

Chapter 13
Ralph Waldo Emerson

Ralph Waldo Emerson (1803-1882)

As an American essayist, poet, and popular philosopher, Ralph Waldo Emerson began his career as a Unitarian minister in Boston, but achieved worldwide fame as a lecturer and the author of such essays as *Self-Reliance*, *History*, *The Over-Soul*, and *Fate*. Drawing on English and German Romanticism, Neoplatonism, Kantianism, and Hinduism, Emerson developed a metaphysics of process, an epistemology of moods, and an "existentialist" ethics of self-improvement. He influenced generations of Americans, from his friend Henry David Thoreau to John Dewey, and in Europe, Friedrich Nietzsche, who takes up such Emersonian themes as power, fate, the uses of poetry and history, and the critique of Christianity.[①]

[①] https://plato.stanford.edu/entries/emerson/.

Critical Perspectives

1. Psychological Study

Emily Dalton, in "An Unexpected Epigraph: Exploring the Personal and Philosophical Relevance of Ralph Waldo Emerson to Carl Ransom Rogers", points out that "In 1951, Carl Rogers wrote his third major book, *Client-Centered Therapy*, 'a mature presentation of the nondirective and related points of view in counselling and therapy'". "This article takes as the starting point the Emerson epigraph chosen by Rogers for his seminal book *Client-Centered Therapy*, and discovers that Rogers also acknowledged the 'deep influence' that Emerson and the transcendental school had on his personal life and philosophy. It proposes evidence of this influence, noticing similarities in the writings and biographical details of the two men. It also extrapolates a question and proposes it for further research—the possibility that Rogers integrated Emersonian thinking into the development of the person-approach. The limited and interpretive reasoning for such an extrapolation is acknowledged". The article concludes that Emerson was one of many writers in literature, theology, philosophy, psychology, art and science with whom Rogers engaged over his lifetime, an eclectic contributed to Rogers' fluid, ongoing, and ever-evolving creative synthesis. It also concludes that the question of whether Rogers' use of the epigraph at the beginning of *Client-Centered Therapy* indicates a connection between Emerson and Rogers' person-centered theory, is worthy of being asked. [1]

Robinson Woodward-Burns, in "Rethinking Self-Reliance: Emerson on Mobbing, War, and Abolition", presents that as "A famous proponent of solitude and self-reliance, Ralph Waldo Emerson rejected the conformity of Jacksonian mobs and mass parties for solitary nature walks, and so has long been read as an antipolitical figure. Recent scholars have reinterpreted Emersonian self-reliance to include extralegal boycotts of slave-made goods and resistance to the Fugitive Slave Act. This essay takes these accounts a step further, arguing that Emerson saw that some forms of extralegal cooperative action were compatible with self-reliance. Specifically, self-reliance requires contemplating and then acting on personal moral rules. As Northern crowds rallied to rescue and harbor fugitive slaves, Emerson saw that joining an abolitionist

---

[1] Dalton E. "An Unexpected Epigraph: Exploring the Personal and Philosophical Relevance of Ralph Waldo Emerson to Carl Ransom Rogers". Person-Centered and Experiential Psychotherapies, 2022, 21(3): 235-249.

crowd allowed unconventional debate and intellectual self-reliance and created a space to act on one's personal principles, encouraging active self-reliance. Union enlistment similarly let free Blacks and antislavery Northerners enact their principles and achieve a measure of self-reliance. Paradoxically, self-reliance can sometimes be achieved through common action".①

Susan Field, in "Open to Influence: Ralph Waldo Emerson and Audre Lorde on Loss", examines the similarities in language, emotion, philosophical creativity, and purpose which exist between Ralph Waldo Emerson's remarks about his son Waldo's death and Audre Lorde's remarks about her breast cancer. Both writers experienced and thought about their losses for the rest of their lives. One such loss specific to the work of Emerson and Lorde is the restriction of personal mourning in favor of socially acceptable grieving behavior. Both Emerson and Lorde pursue the expression of their grief as a contribution to a public discussion of the problem of losing individuality in the U.S., a problem tantamount to losing the contribution of the individual artist/thinker/critic in favor of societal interests deeply connected to corporate profit for Lorde and to deadening conformity for Emerson. Profound and perhaps unbridgeable differences loom between Emerson and Lorde across chasms of race and sex, of sexuality and political engagement, of era and temperament. The raw bewilderment and bitterness in the letters and journals ripen to fruitful inquiries about losing and finding in their public expressions. Both Emerson and Lorde conceive of power as acting on the experiential knowledge of irreducible difference, whether the innavigable difference death creates between father and son despite the ties of love and blood or the severance of flesh from flesh rendered by the surgical knife. For both writers, movement is the universal sign of life.②

Sanford Pinsker, in "Was Ralph Waldo Emerson Our First Motivational Speaker?", explores whether Ralph Waldo Emerson could be considered the first motivational speaker in the United States. Topics discussed include examples of his quotable maxims, and distinction of Emerson from other motivational speakers.③

Joseph M. Kramp, in "From Emerson to Erikson: Methodological Reflections on a Common, Anti-American Approach to Biography", presents an examination into the methodological similarities shared by the 19th-century American transcendentalist Ralph Waldo Emerson and the 20th-century German American psychologist Erik H. Erikson in regard to their interest in biography as a genre. Details are given describing Emerson's interest in biography writing against previous U.S. literary conventions which avoided the depiction of psychological pain and

---

① Woodward-Burns R. "Rethinking Self-Reliance: Emerson on Mobbing, War, and Abolition". The Journal of Politics, 2021, 83(1): 137-149.
② Field S. "Open to Influence: Ralph Waldo Emerson and Audre Lorde on Loss". American Transcendental Quarterly, 2005, 19(1): 5-22.
③ Pinsker S. "Was Ralph Waldo Emerson Our First Motivational Speaker?". The Virginia Quarterly Review, 2001, 77(3): 509-513.

weakness, similarities seen in the writing techniques of both Emerson and Erikson, and how Emerson's biographical writings can be seen as seeking the resolution of life cycle crises as theorized by Erikson.[①]

Joseph M. Kramp, in "Emerson's Masculinity Conflict", focuses on the American essayist and poet Ralph Waldo Emerson, his internal conflict regarding his sexual orientation and how it influenced his resignation from the pastorate in 1832. The author provides three arguments in defense of his assertion regarding Emerson's masculinity conflict and its impact on his resignation. The author expands on these three arguments, including the psychological aspects of Emerson's interpersonal relations with his family as an adolescent, his compliant behaviors with his aunt and siblings, and the significance of his post-ministry moratorium in his development as an adult.[②]

2. Religious Study

Ann Beebe, in "'Light Is the First of Painters': Ralph Waldo Emerson and the Luminism of John Frederick Kensett", points out that in addition to encouraging nineteenth-century authors, the essays of Ralph Waldo Emerson served as an inspiration to American artists. This essay examines three affinities between Emerson's prose (Nature and "Art") and the artwork of John Frederick Kensett, with a focus on Kensett's *Lake George*. The landscapist and the painting appear to embody Christian expectations for character, duty, and faith as articulated by the essayist.[③]

Russell C. Powell, in "Shame, Moral Motivation, and Climate Change", suggests that an emotion like shame is endowed with special motivational force. "Drawing on Ralph Waldo Emerson's concept of shame, I develop an account of moral motivation that lends new perspective to the contemporary climate crisis. Whereas religious ethicists often engage the problem of climate change by re-imagining the metaphors, symbols, and values of problematic cosmologies, I focus on some specific moral tactics generated by religious communities who use their traditions to confront climate destruction. In particular, Bartimaeus Cooperative Ministries, a Christian non-profit organization that seeks to infuse a renewed commitment in church parishes to bioregions and watersheds, effectively employs shame in the context of its Christian practice and leadership. My analysis of Bartimaeus Cooperative Ministries demonstrates both the

---

① Kramp J M. "From Emerson to Erikson: Methodological Reflections on a Common, Anti-American Approach to Biography". Journal of Psychohistory, 2013, 41(1): 44-51.
② Kramp J M. "Emerson's Masculinity Conflict". Journal of Psychohistory, 2012, 40(1): 21-31.
③ Beebe A. "'Light Is the First of Painters': Ralph Waldo Emerson and the Luminism of John Frederick Kensett". Religion and the Arts, 2019, 23(5): 467-488.

efficacy of shame to motivate environmentally responsible behavior as well as the advantage to religious ethics of considering contextual practices over abstract cosmologies". [1]

Emily Dumler-Winckler, in "Emersonian Virtues of the Anthropocene: Faith, Hope, and Love", argues that "The natural sciences and religion are two of the primary modern social practices that, for better and worse, shape our relationship to nature. Ralph Waldo Emerson helps us to think about their relation to one another and the virtues needed for the perfection of each. His insights about virtue and the 'religious sentiment' shed light on how we moderns might make a home of a world indelibly marked by science, technology, and anthropogenic change. In addition to the quintessentially Emersonian virtue of self-trust, the virtues of faith, hope, and love are vital for this home-making endeavor. Emerson, thus, prefigures what prominent environmental ethicists have described as a 'turn to virtue in climate ethics', as well as what some see as a return to religious communities, values, and ideals, as the way forward. By guiding readers through Emerson's early work *Nature* and his late essay *Worship*, this article provides an account of these three traditionally theological Emersonian virtues of the Anthropocene". [2]

Charles Stang, in "Flesh and Fire: Incarnation and Deification in Origen of Alexandria", offers two models for understanding Origen of Alexandria's theological anthropology, Christology, and soteriology. According to the first, the fiery mind is encased in a soul and a body for its earthly sojourn, but will eventually shed both. According to the second, soul and body are understood as the fiery mind in different "states of matter"; neither is shed, but rather transformed to its original condition— "all flesh must once again become fire". The second model is explored and ultimately endorsed, in dialogue with Ralph Waldo Emerson and T. S. Eliot. This model had implications for how we understand embodiment, temporality, rehabilitation, and the final restoration of all things (apokatastasis). [3]

Clare Elliott, in "'A Backward Glance O'er' the (Dis)United States: William Blake, Ralph Waldo Emerson and the 'Authentic American Religion'", begins with a brief consideration of the resurgence of religious rhetoric used by George W. Bush. It discusses this alongside what Harold Bloom terms an "authentic American religion" in his article. Bloom looks retrospectively at Emersonian self-reliance as the "authentic American religion" and he urges contemporary American readers to remember this as a truly American religion. An exploration of this apparent correlation between self-reliance and an authentic American religion uncovers the somewhat unnoticed influence of William Blake's poetry on Ralph Waldo Emerson's essays. A close

---

[1] Powell R C. "Shame, Moral Motivation, and Climate Change". Worldviews: Global Religions, Culture and Ecology, 2019, 23(3): 230-253.
[2] Dumler-Winckler E. "Emersonian Virtues of the Anthropocene: Faith, Hope, and Love". Zygon: Journal of Religion and Science, 2018, 53(4): 971-991.
[3] Stang C. "Flesh and Fire: Incarnation and Deification in Origen of Alexandria". Adamantius, 2019(25): 123-132.

analysis of Emerson's early reading of Blake beside a consideration of Blake's *London* (1794), *The Clod and the Pebble* (1794) and Emerson's *Self-Reliance* (1841) and *Society and Solitude* (1870) documents the development of Emersonian self-reliance into a more assured term. This is accounted for by Emerson's growing interest and immersion in the poetry of this English poet, William Blake. The article concludes, contentiously, with the declaration that it is only through this transatlantic study of Blake's and Emerson's writing that Bloom's "authentic American religion" can really be understood. [①]

David L. Smith, in "'The Sphinx Must Solve Her Own Riddle': Emerson, Secrecy, and the Self-Reflexive Method", offers a fresh approach to the religious thought of Ralph Waldo Emerson, exploring the particular conception of secrecy in connection with which he understands the human spiritual predicament, and his response to this predicament by means of a self-reflexive turn in his writing—a procedure designed to undermine quests for truth elsewhere and so to restore the self to the wholeness implicit in its initial conditions. The operation of this method is traced through a number of Emerson's major works, including *Nature*, *History*, and the poem *The Sphinx*. Along the way, Emerson's thought is discussed in relation to the history of Emerson criticism, alternative views of secrecy in religion, and the theory and practice of religious nondualism, to which Emerson's intellectual project bears considerable resemblance. [②]

Martin Kevorkian, in "A Pulpit of Envy: Girardian Elements in Emerson's Last 'Supper'", discusses the Lord's Supper Controversy, an aspect of the career of writer Ralph Waldo Emerson, in light of sermons that Emerson preached at the time. The thought of literary theorist René Girard is addressed in relation to the role of envy in Emerson's sermons, which focus on the life of religious figure Jesus Christ. [③]

Jonathan Bishop, in "Emerson and Christianity", examines the role of Ralph Waldo Emerson in Christianity. Topics discussed include Emerson's approach towards Christianity; natural history of intellect as Emerson's most persistent concerns; and sources of Emerson's belief in the moral sentiment as at once inborn and infinite. [④]

Robin Sandra Grey, in "'A Seraph's Eloquence': Emerson's Inspired Language and Milton's Apocalyptic Prose", examines the influence of John Milton's apocalyptic prose tracts on the works of Ralph Waldo Emerson. Topics discussed include power of efficacious language to devastate and cleanse; divine rewards of true eloquence; portrayal of a God both unimaginably magnificent and inscrutable; release from spiritual and epistemological blindness; and

---

① Elliott C. "'A Backward Glance O'er' the (Dis)United States: William Blake, Ralph Waldo Emerson and the 'Authentic American Religion'". European Journal of American Culture, 2009, 28(1): 75-93.
② Smith D L. "'The Sphinx Must Solve Her Own Riddle': Emerson, Secrecy, and the Self-Reflexive Method". Journal of the American Academy of Religion, 2003, 71(4): 835-861.
③ Kevorkian M. "A Pulpit of Envy: Girardian Elements in Emerson's Last 'Supper'". Renascence, 1999, 52(1): 89-104.
④ Bishop J. "Emerson and Christianity". Renascence, 1998, 50(3/4): 220-237.

correspondence between the voices of conscience and recrimination.[1]

P. Eddy Wilson, in "Emerson and Dewey on Natural Piety", explores the ways that natural piety would be expressed if one adopted the naturalism of Ralph Waldo Emerson and John Dewey. Topics discussed include Emerson's and Dewey's views of nature and natural piety; practical activity and practical reasoning; and entailments of applied natural piety.[2]

3. New Historicism Study

Adam H. Hines, in "Ralph Waldo Emerson and Oliver Wendell Holmes, Jr.: The Subtle Rapture of Postponed Power", discusses the 19th century American philosopher Ralph Waldo Emerson's influence on the U.S. Supreme Court Justice Oliver Wendell Holmes Jr.'s (Junior's) legal philosophy, including Holmes' perspective on legal realism. The impact of Emerson on Holmes' view of the posthumous, or postponed, power of the philosopher through written word is discussed.[3]

G. M. Johnson, in "Ralph Waldo Emerson on Isaac Hecker: A Manuscript with Commentary", presents and analyzes the recorded reactions on the encounters between writers Ralph Waldo Emerson and Isaac Hecker as seen in the unpublished manuscript "Hecker, and the Catholic Church". Subjects addressed include the tone of Emerson's statement about Hecker, Hecker's tendency to set up Emerson as an intellectual opponent, and Hecker's surprise over Emerson's hostility.[4]

Scott Holland, in "The Poet, Theopoetics, and Theopolitics", explores the influence of the theopoetics of philosopher Ralph Waldo Emerson on poet Walt Whitman and Transcendentalist author Moncure Daniel Conway. The author reflects on the radicalism of Whitman and the religious aspects of the book *Leaves of Grass* which explore the themes of body and soul. Other topics include the task of self-creation, abolitionism, and the essay *Circles*.[5]

Jeffrey Einboden, in "The Early American Qur'an: Islamic Scripture and US Canon", suggests that although considerable scholarly attention has been paid to US Orientalism in the nineteenth century, there remains no targeted study of the formative influence exercised by the

---

[1] Grey R S. "'A Seraph's Eloquence': Emerson's Inspired Language and Milton's Apocalyptic Prose". Modern Philology, 1994, 92(1): 36-63.

[2] Wilson P E. "Emerson and Dewey on Natural Piety". The Journal of Religion, 1995, 75(3): 329-346.

[3] Hines A H. "Ralph Waldo Emerson and Oliver Wendell Holmes, Jr.: The Subtle Rapture of Postponed Power". Journal of Supreme Court History, 2019, 44(1): 39-52.

[4] Johnson G M. "Ralph Waldo Emerson on Isaac Hecker: A Manuscript with Commentary". The Catholic Historical Review, 1993, 79(1): 54-64.

[5] Holland S. "The Poet, Theopoetics, and Theopolitics". Cross-Currents: East Asian History and Culture Review, 2014, 64 (4): 496-508.

Qur'an upon the canon of early American literature. This paper surveys receptions, adaptations and translations of the Qur'an during the American Renaissance, identifying the Qur'anic echoes which permeate the seminal works of literary patriarchs such as Ralph Waldo Emerson, Washington Irving and Edgar Allan Poe. Examining the literary and religious tensions raised by antebellum importations of Islamic scripture, the essay interrogates how the aesthetic contours of the Qur'an in particular serve both to attract and obstruct early US readings, mapping the diverse responses to the Muslim sacred generated by American Romantics and Transcendentalists.①

John-Charles Duffy, in "'A Religion by Revelation': Emerson as Radical Restorationist", argues that poet Ralph Waldo Emerson has engaged in a mode of religious discourse called "radical restorationism". Topics discussed include a historical overview of restorationism in the United States; characteristics of radical restorationism that underlie Mormonism; and outcome of his prophetic career.②

Lucy Pearce, in "Re-visioning History: Countering Emerson's Alleged Ahistoricity", suggests that "Just as 'man is explicable by nothing less than his entire history', so Emerson's ideas on history need the context of their own history—the influence of European Romantic developments and interest in history and New England Puritanism. Emerson has been dismissed by many as ahistorical; yet, history is one of the cornerstones of the Emersonian world view—an abstract, dry shell of a concept he seeks to redefine as something vital". His attitudes towards history are indicative of his broader push to break with tradition, approach human and cultural needs afresh and empower the American Individual.③

4. Ethical Study

Ryan W. Davis, in "Frontier Kantianism: Autonomy and Authority in Ralph Waldo Emerson and Joseph Smith", presents that "Ralph Waldo Emerson is often seen as the early American prophet of autonomy. This essay suggests a perhaps surprising fellow traveler in this prophetic call: Joseph Smith. Smith opposed religious creeds for the same reason that Emerson denounced them, namely that creeds represent a threat to the autonomy of a person's beliefs. Smith and Emerson also forward similar defenses of individual autonomy in action. Furthermore, they encounter a shared problem: how can autonomy be possible in a society where other

---

① Einboden J. "The Early American Qur'an: Islamic Scripture and US Canon". Journal of Qur'anic Studies, 2009, 11(2): 1-19.

② Duffy J-C. "'A Religion by Revelation': Emerson as Radical Restorationist". American Quarterly Transcendental, 2000, 14(3): 227-250.

③ Pearce L. "Re-visioning History: Countering Emerson's Alleged Ahistoricity". European Journal of American Culture, 2007, 26(1): 41-56.

individuals hold some kind of authority? I propose that each thinker resolves this tension through an insight with a Kantian echo. A suitably qualified version of authority can sometimes count as an expression of, rather than hindrance to, autonomy. I describe the overlap in Emerson and Smith as a 'frontier' version of Kantianism. They favor determining one's own beliefs and actions in a way that looks forward to an open future of possibility". [1]

5. Philosophical Study

Harold Fromm, in "Overcoming the Oversoul: Emerson's Evolutionary Existentialism", presents his experience of reading and teaching the works of Ralph Waldo Emerson, and how his view of Emerson has changed over time. Topics discussed include discussion of a selection of books about Emerson; reaction of other professors to Emerson's work; and various views of the philosophies espoused by Emerson. [2]

Douglas R. Anderson, in "American Loss in Cavell's Emerson", comments on the literary work of philosopher Stanley Cavell redeeming author Ralph Waldo Emerson as philosopher. Topics discussed include ways in which philosophers gave power to the work of Emerson in U.S. culture; forgetfulness with which connectedness has been met by philosophers and intellectual historians; and method of artistic thinking as a paradigm for intelligence. [3]

David Larocca, in "Not Following Emerson: Intelligibility and Identity in the Authorship of Literature, Science, and Philosophy", suggests that "The case of Emerson's reception—or the points of resistance it reveals—in the intellectual culture he helped found reminds readers in any discipline that criteria frame an interpretation even while it is being made. The diversity of opinion about the nature of Emerson's writing prompts a reader's wider concern about the intelligibility and identity of the text under examination. Do I understand it? And what is it, anyway? As shown Laura Otis's anthology of works in literature and science pressed up beside one another, there are times when the negotiated boundaries of thought are meaningfully apparent. Emerson's nineteenth century was such a time, and Emerson's writing was such a space for exploring those boundaries and definitions. When those liminal spaces are filled and sometimes ossify, possibilities for reading are narrowed or confounded. If the ongoing dominance of natural science, mostly by reason of its empirical success, has eclipsed innovations in the literary, historical, and philosophical arts, the varied reading of Emerson's work by critics—

---

[1] Davis R W. "Frontier Kantianism: Autonomy and Authority in Ralph Waldo Emerson and Joseph Smith". The Journal of Religious Ethics, 2018, 46(2): 332-359.

[2] Fromm H. "Overcoming the Oversoul: Emerson's Evolutionary Existentialism". The Hudson Review, 2004, 57(1): 71-95.

[3] Anderson D R. "American Loss in Cavell's Emerson". Transactions of the Charles S. Peirce Society, 1993, 29(1): 69-89.

even up to the present day—suggests that we still inhabit an age of negotiation and discovery".①

Martin A. Coleman, in "Emerson's 'Philosophy of the Street'", discusses the traditional interpretation of the work of Ralph Waldo Emerson that portrays him as a champion of nature, wilderness or country life and an opponent of the city, technology or urban life. Topics discussed include conflict in his views on the city and nature; background on his emergence as an anti-urban philosopher; and value of natural objects in harmony with spiritual activity.②

Jeffrey Downard, in "Emerson's Experimental Ethics and Kant's Analysis of Beauty", argues that Ralph Waldo Emerson has developed a rich philosophical position over the course of his writings as opposed to the claim of Immanuel Kant that Emerson's essays were beautiful but shallow. Topics discussed include comparison of the ideas in the ethics of Emerson with the aesthetics of Kant; stance of Emerson on humanity and morality; analysis of Emerson's account of spontaneous judgments and the analysis of aesthetic judgments of the beautiful by Kant.③

Erin E. Flynn, in "Intellectual Intuition in Emerson and the Early German Romantics", presents insights on Ralph Waldo Emerson's romantic conceptions of intellectual intuition and the early German romantics. It mentions that Emerson opposed Immanuel Kant's denial of intellectual intuition. It examines some sections in the last part of *Critique of Judgment* by Kant to decipher the alleged implications. It concludes two criticisms in the thoughts of Emerson: epistemological and the virtue in romantic fixation.④

Shari Goldberg, in "From Quietism to Quiet Politics: Inheriting Emerson's Antislavery Testimony", argues that "While Ralph Waldo Emerson has been increasingly acknowledged as an American thinker influential in the evolution of nineteenth-century philosophy, his essays have largely failed to escape the charges of quietism and political apathy bestowed upon them in his lifetime. Yet if Emerson insisted on the importance of silence to the antislavery movement, it was perhaps due to his theory that one's deepest obligations become involuntarily part of the self and thus refuse to withstand representation in direct speech. My article reads Emerson's writing in this light, suggesting more broadly that the common notion that silence and politics are antithetical be reconsidered with regard to the possibility that what constitutes political speech need not be explicit — or even vocal".⑤

---

① Larocca D. "Not Following Emerson: Intelligibility and Identity in the Authorship of Literature, Science, and Philosophy". The Midwest Quarterly, 2013, 54(2): 115-135.
② Coleman M A. "Emerson's 'Philosophy of the Street'". Transactions of the Charles S. Peirce Society, 2000, 36(2): 271-283.
③ Downard J. "Emerson's Experimental Ethics and Kant's Analysis of Beauty". Transactions of the Charles S. Peirce Society, 2003, 39(1): 87-112.
④ Flynn E E. "Intellectual Intuition in Emerson and the Early German Romantics". The Philosophical Forum, 2009, 40(3): 367-389.
⑤ Goldberg S. "From Quietism to Quiet Politics: Inheriting Emerson's Antislavery Testimony". Paragraph, 2008, 31(3): 281-303.

Christopher Leise, in "The Eye-ball and the Butterfly: Beauty and the Individual Soul in Emerson and Hawthorne", discusses the concept of private selfhood as articulated in Ralph Waldo Emerson's and Nathaniel Hawthorne's writing about beauty. Topics discussed include Emerson and Hawthorne's competing definitions of beauty; the distinctions between Emerson's and Hawthorne's idea of a self's fullest realization; and the parallels between the two thinkers' notion of beauty and virtues.[①]

Claudia Schumann, in "Aversive Education: Emersonian Variations on 'Bildung'", discusses "Ralph Waldo Emerson's thought in relation to the German Bildung tradition. For many, Bildung still signifies a valuable achievement of modern educational thought as well as a critical, emancipatory ideal which, frequently in a rather nostalgic manner, is appealed to in order to delineate problematic tendencies of current educational trends. Others, in an at times rather cynical manner, claim that Bildung through its successful institutionalization has shaped vital features of our present educational system and has thus served its time and lost its critical potential. When thinking through Emerson's variations on Bildung, I argue against the nostalgic appeals to Bildung that the criticism against it has to be taken seriously. Against the cynical assessment of Bildung having run its course, I will hold that with Emerson we can develop the idea of an 'aversive education' as a call for Bildung to be turned upon itself, allowing to revive it as a conceptual tool for transformation, drawing particular attention to its political dimension".[②]

David Greenham, in "'Altars to the Beautiful Necessity': The Significance of F. W. J. Schelling's *Philosophical Inquiries in the Nature of Human Freedom* in the Development of Ralph Waldo Emerson's Concept of Fate", discusses the influence that the German philosopher F. W. J. Schelling's 1809 book *Philosophical Inquiries into the Nature of Human Freedom* had on the American transcendentalist philosopher Ralph Waldo Emerson's conception of fate. Emerson's perspective on free will is discussed.[③]

Emily Dumler-Winckler, in "Can Genius Be Taught? Emerson's Genius and the Virtues of Modern Science", considers Emerson's claim "Genius, cannot be taught', and explores its significance for moral education, specifically in modern science, by focusing on Emerson's account of genius and the virtue of self-trust that perfects it. Genius, for Emerson, does not refer only to extraordinary works or persons. It is also the creative action of the soul to be cultivated by all. Self-trust, in which all the virtues are realized, is its chief virtue. Emerson knows that virtue

---

① Leise C. "The Eye-ball and the Butterfly: Beauty and the Individual Soul in Emerson and Hawthorne". Philological Quarterly, 2013, 92(4): 471-497.
② Schumann C. "Aversive Education: Emersonian Variations on 'Bildung'". Educational Philosophy and Theory, 2019, 51 (5): 488-497.
③ Greenham D. "'Altars to the Beautiful Necessity': The Significance of F. W. J. Schelling's *Philosophical Inquiries in the Nature of Human Freedom* in the Development of Ralph Waldo Emerson's Concept of Fate". Journal of the History of Ideas, 2015, 76(1): 115-137.

begins but does not end in imitation. The goal of moral education is not simply to ape the virtues of those we love and admire, but to cultivate the virtues needed to innovate on received models, to excel by pressing beyond exemplars who have gone before. Can genius, then, be taught? Emerson's answer is not so simple as it may appear at first blush.①

William J. Berger, in "A Sympathetic Reading of Emerson's Politics", focuses on the challenge of interpreting Ralph Waldo Emerson's political philosophy due to his inward-directed writings, despite he is considered by some as a philosopher of democracy. It explores how individuals can form social and political bonds through affective capacities, resonating with contemporary political theory emphasizing the role of emotions in politics, using J. D. Salinger's life as an illustration of an Emersonian political agent.②

Nell Irvin Painter, in "Ralph Waldo Emerson's Saxons", discusses "Anglo-Saxonism", or glorification of the Anglo-Saxon heritage of Americans, in the thought of 19th-century American writer and philosopher Ralph Waldo Emerson. The evolution of racial or proto-racial thinking about whiteness and white people in the United States is discussed, beginning with U. S. president Thomas Jefferson's admiration for the Anglo-Saxons of England. Also mentioned is Emerson's mentor, the Scottish writer Thomas Carlyle, who has written about the bonds of Anglo-Saxon kinship between Britons and Americans. Emerson's book *English Traits* (1856), lauding the strong masculine characteristics of the English, said to be inherited from their Saxon ancestors, is also discussed.③

David Heddendorf, in "What Is Emerson for?", analyzes the essays by U.S. writer, poet and essayist Ralph Waldo Emerson. Topics covered include his essays about Old World experience and American idealism. Also discussed are Emerson's Transcendentalism movement and his theories of symbolism.④

Algis Valiunas, in "Ralph Waldo Emerson, Big Talker", presents a critique of the author and philosopher Ralph Waldo Emerson. His reputation as a wise and kind man who labored to promote a distinctively American understanding of greatness is noted, and some biographical information is included. Emerson's essays such as *The Over-Soul* and *Heroism* are discussed, and a tension in his thought between the desire to promote intellectualism among the masses, and the desire to valorize exceptional individuals are analyzed.⑤

John Michael Corrigan, in "The Metempsychotic Mind: Emerson and Consciousness", considers nineteenth century American philosopher and author Ralph Waldo Emerson, focusing

---

① Dumler-Winckler E. "Can Genius Be Taught? Emerson's Genius and the Virtues of Modern Science". Journal of Moral Education, 2018, 47(1):1-17.
② Berger W J. "A Sympathetic Reading of Emerson's Politics". Humanitas, 2019, 32(1/2): 105-124.
③ Painter N I. "Ralph Waldo Emerson's Saxons". The Journal of American History, 2009, 1995(4): 977-985.
④ Heddendorf D. "What Is Emerson for?". The Sewanee Review, 2016, 124(3): 482-488.
⑤ Valiunas A. "Ralph Waldo Emerson, Big Talker". Commentary, 2010, 130(2): 55-58.

particularly on Emerson's ideas regarding metempsychosis, or transmigration of the soul. The author argues that Emerson's study of ancient Greek philosophy, Confucianism, and Hinduism has led to his adoption of beliefs in religious universals, including transmigration of the soul. Emerson would have seen such a continuity of an individual as being important to the development of history and the creation of self. The author also discusses the historiography of Emerson studies and transcendentalism.[1]

Ryan White, in "Neither Here nor There: On Grief and Absence in Emerson's *Experience*", presents a literary criticism of the essay *Experience*, by Ralph Waldo Emerson. It says that the essay is notable, for it shows the refusal of Emerson to display his grief when his young son died, and refers to his son in the essay as "my son". It refers to the analysis by Sharon Cameron to Emerson's essay in her own influential essay *Representing Grief: Emerson's "Experience"*, wherein she interprets the grief of Emerson. It explores the philosophical concepts in *Experience* through metaphysical study.[2]

Richard Poirier, in "An Approach to Unapproachable America", discusses a passage in Ralph Waldo Emerson's essay *Experience*. A discussion is presented about Emerson's writings and previous attempts to interpret *Experience*. The author focuses on Emerson's thoughts on dualism and his journey into the "unapproachable America" described in the essay. The article describes the essay's narrator as a guide into a pastoral landscape. The author's response to *Experience* is presented, along with a discussion about the problems faced by literary critics trying to analyze the essay.[3]

Matthew W. DeVoll, in "Emerson and Dreams: Toward a Natural History of Intellect", examines writer Ralph Waldo Emerson's notions of dreams. "From his early years of Transcendentalism in the 1830s to the waning years of his active intellectual life in the 1870s, Emerson privately and publicly speculates on the strange wisdom of dreams". In the development of his natural history of intellect, Emerson reflects uneasily on the apparently daemonic nature of dreams. In his lecture, Emerson confesses his trepidation before dreams. Emerson struggles to put dreams intellectually and morally underfoot by explaining their source and nature and distilling their energy for a practical, ethical purpose. He insists that dreams have a certain nature and reason, in that they illustrate the unplumbed structure of the intellect and its double-consciousness. Dreams for Emerson pertain to a mysterious structural force of the self, what he at times refers to as the unconscious mind. While Emerson insists that evolutionary law presides over the dreaming unconscious, whose end is the idealized intellect, Demonology

---

[1] Corrigan J M. "The Metempsychotic Mind: Emerson and Consciousness". Journal of the History of Ideas, 2010, 71(3): 433-455.

[2] White R. "Neither Here nor There: On Grief and Absence in Emerson's *Experience*". The Journal of Speculative Philosophy, 2009, 23(4): 285-306.

[3] Poirier R. "An Approach to Unapproachable America". Raritan, 2007, 26(4): 1-13.

suggests that his faith in order may not be purely affirmative in its origin.①

John Lysaker, in "Relentless Unfolding: Emerson's Individual", discusses eight theses that any successful reconstruction must embrace. "I am not claiming that these theses are unique to Emerson; others hold similar views. I have elected to work with Emerson, however, because his work eludes the exhausted opposition between atomistic and collectivist accounts of human flourishing". "Emersonian individualism remains a living project, one we would do well to understand more thoroughly and pursue more rigorously". Additional topics discussed include living nature of Emersonian individualism; emerson's denial of the possibility of an atomistic self; characterization of Emerson as a "salutary interlocutor for those who would rethink individualism"; and dialectical nature of individuation.②

6. Post-colonial Study

Dean Flower, in "Of Shanties and Slavery", focuses on the life of essayist Ralph Waldo Emerson and the association between shanties and slavery. Topics discussed include the life of Emerson, his purchase of land, his thoughts about the possession of land, the memoirs and biographies of some authors about Emerson, and some issues on slavery in shanties.③

Jack Turner, in "Emerson, Slavery, and Citizenship", offers a counter argument to the ideas that Ralph Waldo Emerson is not a voice of social or civic responsibility. The author shows that Emerson's advocacy of the self-reliant individual is a fundamental aspect of what a democracy is founded on. These are people who hold themselves and their governments responsible for their actions. The author examines Emerson's essays that deal with slavery in the United States in order to show his conceptualization of citizenship.④

Marek Paryz, in "Beyond the Traveler's Testimony: Emerson's *English Traits* and the Construction of Postcolonial Counter-Discourse", examines the book *English Traits*, by Ralph Waldo Emerson, and its role in the efforts of the author to give testimony to the growing power of the U.S. and the maturation of the American national consciousness in the context of Anglo-American travel writing. In the book, Emerson used a multi-faceted presentation of England to encode his vision of the U.S. The technique implies that the author is still concerned with the country's colonial legacy. The novel presents several connected aspects of the traveler's

---

① DeVoll M W. "Emerson and Dreams: Toward a Natural History of Intellect". American Transcendental Quarterly, 2004, 18(2): 69-87.
② Lysaker J. "Relentless Unfolding: Emerson's Individual". The Journal of Speculative Philosophy, 2003, 17(3): 155-163.
③ Flower D. "Of Shanties and Slavery". The Hudson Review, 2018, 71(1): 15-25.
④ Turner J. "Emerson, Slavery, and Citizenship". Raritan, 2008, 28(2): 127-146.

discourse which have important political implications.[1]

Peter S. Field, in "The Strange Career of Emerson and Race", points out that "Ralph Waldo Emerson, the nineteenth century's greatest American liberal thinker, was, along with Frederick Douglass, the most important intellectual to engage the race issue. Friend of John Brown, collaborator with Garrison and Phillips, peripheral participant in the Underground Railroad, Emerson nevertheless remained conflicted about many issues relating to race and the character of the American nation". This essay seeks to explain the trajectory of Emerson's antislavery commitments as well as the developments of his broader political thought in the context of his evolving views on race. A close scrutiny of Emerson's racial prejudices reveals how in critical ways they circumscribe his larger social and political thought and limit his actions. Additional topics include details on the first phase of the evolving views of Emerson on race and slavery; transformation in rethinking the relationship of slavery and race; and position on abolitionism after 1850.[2]

Amy E. Earhart, in "Representative Men, Slave Revolt, and Emerson's 'Conversion' to Abolitionism", deals with the writings of American writer Ralph Waldo Emerson on the issues of slavery and abolition in the United States. Topics discussed include reference to Len Gougeon's book *Virtue's Hero: Emerson, Antislavery, and Reform*; views of Emerson on suffrage; and opinion on one of Emerson's speeches.[3]

7. Comparative Study

Edward H. Madden, in "Ralph Waldo Emerson and Theodore Parker: A Comparative Study", argues that Ralph Waldo Emerson and Theodore Parker are much alike in their epistemic commitments and that the deviations of Parker are not inconsistent with the beliefs the two men shared. Topics discussed include beliefs on reason and intuition; opinion of Parker on apriori intuitions; commitment of Parker to higher criticism; and evidence of the idealism of Emerson.[4]

Danny Heitman, in "Our Contemporary, Montaigne", focuses on French essayist Michel de Montaigne and views of essayist Ralph Waldo Emerson on him. It highlights that philosophers

---

[1] Paryz M. "Beyond the Traveler's Testimony: Emerson's *English Traits* and the Construction of Postcolonial Counter-Discourse". American Transcendental Quarterly, 2006, 20(3): 565–590.
[2] Field P S. "The Strange Career of Emerson and Race". American Nineteenth Century History, 2001, 2(1): 1–32.
[3] Earhart A E. "Representative Men, Slave Revolt, and Emerson's 'Conversion' to Abolitionism". American Transcendental Quarterly,1999, 13(4): 287–303.
[4] Madden E H. "Ralph Waldo Emerson and Theodore Parker: A Comparative Study". Transactions of the Charles S. Peirce Society, 1993, 29(2): 179–209.

were inspired by his frank and honest writing, including Emerson and Lewis Thomas. It mentions that Emerson considered Montaigne's essays as the language of conversation which is transferred to a book. It states that Montaigne's essays were revolutionary, and they never went out of print, which was the encouraging aspect of civilization.①

8. Eco-Criticism Study

Sean Ross Meehan, in "Ecology and Imagination: Emerson, Thoreau, and the Nature of Metonymy", explores the works of American authors Ralph Waldo Emerson and Henry David Thoreau, particularly focusing on their treatment of natural and environmental aesthetics in their works. It addresses Thoreau's ecocentrism and Emerson's anthropocentrism, as well as notes the use of metonymy. Works explored include *Nature*, and *Representative Men*, by Emerson and *Walden*, by Thoreau.②

Daniel Payne, in "Emerson's Natural Theology: John Burroughs and the 'Church' of Latter Day Transcendentalism", offers a discussion of American essayist Ralph Waldo Emerson, transcendentalism and natural theology. Natural theology is defined as the belief that human intellect can discover truths about God by studying the natural world. The article claims that essayist John Burroughs's religious opinions reveal him as the key figure in proselytizing for a religion of nature that reconciles the idealistic natural theology of Emerson's transcendentalism with the discoveries of modern science. It explores Emerson's influence on Burroughs and considers Walt Whitman's and Charles Darwin's influences upon the development of Burroughs's philosophy.③

Richard R. O'Keefe, in "The Rats in the Wall: Animals in Emerson's *History*", examines the animal imagery in Ralph Waldo Emerson's essay *History*. Topics discussed include kinds of animals mentioned in the text; appearance of the rat and the lizard in the penultimate paragraph; fear of the encroachment of the animals upon the human; and prelude to the future evolutionary development of animals to higher forms.④

---

① Heitman D. "Our Contemporary, Montaigne". Humanities, 2015, 36(2): 40-44.
② Meehan S R. "Ecology and Imagination: Emerson, Thoreau, and the Nature of Metonymy". Criticism, 2013, 55(2): 299-329.
③ Payne D. "Emerson's Natural Theology: John Burroughs and the 'Church' of Latter Day Transcendentalism". American Transcendental Quarterly, 2007, 21(3): 191-205.
④ O'Keefe R R. "The Rats in the Wall: Animals in Emerson's *History*". American Transcendental Quarterly, 1996, 10(2): 111-121.

9. Aesthetics Study

John Kaag, in "Fatal Courage: How Emerson Helped Me See, as if for the First Time", discusses how the writings of American author Ralph Waldo Emerson have influenced the way he views the world. Topics covered include the sketchbook *Illustrations of the New Philosophy*, which is related to Emerson by American painter and poet Christopher Pearse Cranch; Emerson's book *Nature*; and the way that sight can determine what life is and what it can become.[①]

Edward H. Madden, and Marian C. Madden, in "Transcendental Dimensions of American Art", discuss the influence of transcendentalists Ralph Waldo Emerson and Walt Whitman on painters Robert Henri and John Sloan in the U.S. Topics discussed include similarities and differences of written philosophies of art and the paintings of Henri and Sloan; views of Henri and Sloan on the philosophy of Emerson; and features of the works of Sloan and Henri.[②]

Richard Tuerk, in "Emerson and the Wasting of Beauty: *The Rhodora*", analyzes Ralph Waldo Emerson's view on the importance of beauty to the physical world in his poem *The Rhodora*. Topics discussed include intrinsic value attached to beauty; potential hostility of elements that provide nurture; and discovery of the dynamic relationship between man, nature and God.[③]

10. Canonization Study

Geoffrey C. Howes, in "Emerson's Image in Turn-of-the-Century Austria: The Cases of Kassner, Friedell, and Musil", explores the similarities between the Austrian fin-de-siècle wave and the Ralph Waldo Emerson wave as represented in the works of Rudolf Kassner, Egon Friedell, and Robert Musil. Problems concerning language, ethics, and epistemology manifested in the study of Emerson's literary works correspond to the problems linked to the turn-of-the-century Austria. Among the authors who studied the works of Emerson, Musil was the only one who went further than Kassner and Friedell.[④]

---

① Kaag J. "Fatal Courage: How Emerson Helped Me See, as if for the First Time". The American Scholar, 2021, 90(1): 16-17.
② Madden E H, Madden M C. "Transcendental Dimensions of American Art". Transactions of the Charles S. Peirce Society, 1996, 32(2): 154-180.
③ Tuerk R. "Emerson and the Wasting of Beauty: *The Rhodora*". American Transcendental Quarterly, 1990, 4(1): 5-11.
④ Howes G C. "Emerson's Image in Turn-of-the-Century Austria: The Cases of Kassner, Friedell, and Musil". Modern Austrian Literature, 1989, 22(3/4): 227-240.

11. Biographical Study

Susan L. Robertson, in "Young Emerson and the Mantle of Biography", discusses the method of Ralph Waldo Emerson in using biography and references to historical figures in his sermons in the 18th century. Topics discussed include value of the past in the transformation of the individual, and historical examples of greatness.[①]

[①] Robertson S L. "Young Emerson and the Mantle of Biography". American Transcendental Quarterly, 1991, 5(3): 151-168.

Chapter 14
Henry David Thoreau

Henry David Thoreau (1817-1862)

  Henry David Thoreau was an American philosopher, poet, environmental scientist, and political activist whose major work, *Walden*, draws upon each of these various identities in meditating upon the concrete problems of living in the world as a human being. He sought to revive a conception of philosophy as a way of life, not only a mode of reflective thought and discourse. Thoreau's work was informed by an eclectic variety of sources. He was well-versed in classical Greek and Roman philosophy (and poetry), ranging from the pre-Socratics through the Hellenistic schools, and was also an avid student of the ancient scriptures and wisdom literature of various Asian traditions. He was familiar with modern philosophy ranging from Descartes, Locke, and the Cambridge Platonists through Emerson, Coleridge, and the German Idealists, all of whom are influential on Thoreau's philosophy. In addition to his focus on ethics in an existential spirit, Thoreau also made unique contributions to ontology, the philosophy of science, and radical political thought. Although his political essays have become justly famous, his works on natural science were not even published until the late twentieth century, and they help to give us a more complete picture of him as a thinker.[1]

---

[1] https://plato.stanford.edu/entries/thoreau/.

Critical Perspectives

1. Ecological Study

Frederick C. Lifton, in "Henry Thoreau's Cult(ivation) of Nature: American Landscape and American Self in *Ktaadn* and *Walking*", analyzes the essays *Ktaadn* and *Walking*, by Henry Thoreau and the author's influence on nature lovers and outdoor adventurers. Topics discussed include examination of Thoreau's views on the essence of nature; summary of *Ktaadn*; interpretation of Thoreau's experience on Mount Ktaadn; and redefinition of American social institutions and history.[1]

Daniel C. Dillard, in "Nature, Natural History, and the Dilemma of Religious Liberalism in Thoreau's *The Maine Woods*", explores Henry David Thoreau's "Indian" studies, in particular his widely popular *The Maine Woods*. The author of this article locates Thoreau squarely in nineteenth-century religious liberalism. This allows for a more historicized reading of Thoreau's thinking on nature. "Interplay between religion and natural history in Thoreau's writing unfolded with respect to competing views of nature in nineteenth-century America. In his studies of Maine's Penobscot Indians, Thoreau attempted to wed the natural and supernatural realms. Many nineteenth-century religious liberals engaged in a similar project as they wrestled with their dilemma of whether to salvage or jettison religion as a whole. Instead of signaling a decline in creativity, imagination, or power, Thoreau's substantial research and writing on Native Americans near the end of his life are an indication of important personal and cultural conflicts over the meaning of nature".[2]

Gavin Van Horn, in "Fire on the Mountain: Ecology Gets Its Narrative Totem", argues that "Aldo Leopold's essay *Thinking Like a Mountain* was more than a parable about a redemptive personal moment; it was the fruition of a larger effort on Leopold's part to effectively communicate the fundamentals of a 'land ethic'. I explore striking narrative antecedents to Leopold's 'green fire' moment, including writings by Henry David Thoreau and Ernest Thompson Seton, and articulate why wolves provided the quintessential totem animal for

---

[1] Lifton F C. "Henry Thoreau's Cult(ivation) of Nature: American Landscape and American Self in *Ktaadn* and *Walking*". American Transcendental Quarterly, 1998, 12(1): 67-76.

[2] Dillard D C. "Nature, Natural History, and the Dilemma of Religious Liberalism in Thoreau's *The Maine Woods*". Journal for the Study of Religion, Nature and Culture, 2012, 6(1): 37-55.

communicating a larger ecological 'drama'. Both these literary antecedents and the essay's ongoing—sometimes surprising—impacts are worth exploring, not just because of the high regard in which the essay itself is held but because Leopold succeeded in navigating a problem that persists in our own time: the gap between scientifically informed understandings of the world and effectively communicating those understandings to the public".[1]

Griff Blakewood, in "Nature Mystics and Madmen: Thoreau and Walter Anderson", discusses the similarities between Henry David Thoreau and American watercolorist Walter Inglis Anderson. "In any discussion of naturalists and nature writers who appear to be seeking or to have found a more profound and connected relationship to the natural world, Henry David Thoreau must be considered a central figure, if not the patron saint. Thoreau took the ideas expressed by his Transcendentalist mentors seriously enough to embrace the necessary disciplines and undertake the experiment to determine if transcendentalist ideas held any actual worth to human existence". "To the extent that Zen Buddhism is a valid human response to reality, and to the further extent that Heidegger's philosophical/mythological vision exists as a genuine possibility for creating a Western path to goals shared by Zen, Anderson stands as a monumental, decidedly heroic figure, calling his nihilistic and self-destructive culture back to a meaningful, connected experience of reality".[2]

Jason Gladstone, in "Low-Tech Thoreau; Or, Remediations of the Human in *The Dispersion of Seeds*", explores the representation of the naturalization of the human in the 1862 manuscript *The Dispersion of Seeds* by Henry David Thoreau. It explores the identification of humans, whose ability to perform intentional or purposeful actions differentiates human agency from the agency of the water, animals and wind, as rational subjects. Thoreau also integrates human with nature as a state of continuity that is generated from the reorganizations of actions as operations.[3]

Richard Higgins, in "Thoreau & Trees: A Visceral Connections", features author, naturalist, and poet Henry David Thoreau. It highlights Thoreau's love of trees, which played a significant role in his artistic creativity, philosophical thought, and his inner life. It provides details regarding Thoreau's book *The Maine Woods*, which depicts his connection to trees.[4]

Kenneth Colston, in "A Radical Recalibration of the Moral Economy", focuses on views of philosopher Henry David Thoreau on recalibrating moral economy. Topics discussed include suggestions to achieve economic success by limiting purchase and buying necessary household

---

[1] Van Horn G. "Fire on the Mountain: Ecology Gets Its Narrative Totem". Journal for the Study of Religion, Nature and Culture, 2011, 5(4): 437-464.

[2] Blakewood G. "Nature Mystics and Madmen: Thoreau and Walter Anderson". Interdisciplinary Humanities, 2004, 21/22 (2/1): 195-214.

[3] Gladstone J. "Low-Tech Thoreau; Or, Remediations of the Human in *The Dispersion of Seeds*". Criticism, 2015, 57(3): 349-376.

[4] Higgins R. "Thoreau & Trees: A Visceral Connections". American Forests, 2016, 122(2): 32-39.

items only; role of his book *Walden* in guiding small scale economics; and importance of frugality to recalibrate moral economy by being economical. It also criticizes wage slavery which prohibits a person from enjoying life.[①]

Dianne Timblin, in "Thoreau as Naturalist: A Conversation with Four Authors", presents an interview with several authors, including Richard B. Primack, Richard Higgins and Laura Dassow Walls, on the 19th century American author, naturalist and philosopher Henry David Thoreau. Topics including Primack's book *Walden Warming: Climate Change Comes to Thoreau's Woods*, Higgins' book *Thoreau and the Language of Trees*, and Walls' biography *Henry David Thoreau: A Life*, are discussed.[②]

Richard Primack, Abraham Miller-Rushing, and Tara K. Miller, in "Was Henry David Thoreau a Good Naturalist? An Approach for Assessing Data from Historical Natural History Records", argue that "Ecologists are increasingly combining historical observations made by naturalists with modern observations to detect the ecological effects of climate change. This use of historical observations raises the following question: How do we know that historical data are appropriate to use to answer current ecological questions? In the present article, we address this question for environmental philosopher Henry David Thoreau, author of *Walden*. Should we trust his observations? We qualitatively and quantitatively evaluate Thoreau's observations using a three-step framework. We assess the rigor, accuracy, and utility of his observations to investigate changes in plants and animals over time. We conclude that Thoreau was an accurate observer of nature and a reliable scientist. More importantly, we describe how this simple three-step approach could be used to assess the accuracy of other scientists and naturalists".[③]

Tara K. Miller, Amanda S. Gallinat, Linnea C. Smith, and Richard B. Primack, in "Comparing Fruiting Phenology across Two Historical Datasets: Thoreau's Observations and Herbarium Specimens", present that "Fruiting remains under-represented in long-term phenology records, relative to leaf and flower phenology. Herbarium specimens and historical field notes can fill this gap, but selecting and synthesizing these records for modern-day comparison requires an understanding of whether different historical data sources contain similar information, and whether similar, but not equivalent, fruiting metrics are comparable with one another". "For 67 fleshy-fruited plant species, we compared observations of fruiting phenology made by Henry David Thoreau in Concord, Massachusetts (1850s), with phenology data gathered from herbarium specimens collected across New England (mid-1800s to 2000s). To identify whether fruiting times and the order of fruiting among species are similar between datasets, we compared dates of first, peak and last observed fruiting (recorded by Thoreau), and earliest, mean

---

① Colston K. "A Radical Recalibration of the Moral Economy". The New Oxford Review, 2016, 1983(3): 24-29.
② Timblin D. "Thoreau as Naturalist: A Conversation with Four Authors". American Scientist, 2017, 105(4): 248-251.
③ Primack R, Miller-Rushing A, Miller T K. "Was Henry David Thoreau a Good Naturalist? An Approach for Assessing Data from Historical Natural History Records". BioScience, 2022, 72(10): 1018-1027.

and latest specimen (collected from herbarium records), as well as fruiting durations". "On average, earliest herbarium specimen dates were earlier than first fruiting dates observed by Thoreau; mean specimen dates were similar to Thoreau's peak fruiting dates; latest specimen dates were later than Thoreau's last fruiting dates; and durations of fruiting captured by herbarium specimens were longer than durations of fruiting observed by Thoreau. All metrics of fruiting phenology except duration were significantly, positively correlated within (r: 0.69–0.88) and between (r: 0.59–0.85) datasets". "Strong correlations in fruiting phenology between Thoreau's observations and data from herbaria suggest that field and herbarium methods capture similar broad-scale phenological information, including relative fruiting times among plant species in New England. Differences in the timing of first, last and duration of fruiting suggest that historical datasets collected with different methods, scales and metrics may not be comparable when exact timing is important. Researchers should strongly consider matching methodology when selecting historical records of fruiting phenology for present-day comparisons".[1]

Tracy Fullerton, in "A Year at Play in the Woods of Walden Pond", describes an experience of examining the interactive landscape of Walden Pond in a game translation of Henry David Thoreau's *Walden*. The author of this article reveals her reflections during her visit of the landscape, citing how it has been a simple and satisfying life, and mentions the creation of the video game "Walden, a Game".[2]

Richard Higgins, in "A Transcendentalist at Work", reflects on the home life of essayist, naturalist, poet and philosopher Henry David Thoreau, with a focus on the days he spent in the third-floor garret in his cabin at Walden Pond in Concord, Massachusetts. Topics covered include spareness of his garret compared with the elegance of the main floors of the house, how the garret served as Thoreau's empire where his refuge, library and laboratory can be found, and the thoughts and observations of Thoreau on nature while on his attic.[3]

Ryan Schneider, in "Drowning the Irish: Natural Borders and Class Boundaries in Henry David Thoreau's *Cape Cod*", focuses on narratives of the environment and their relation to dynamics of class depicted in *Cape Cod*, a posthumously-published series of essays which are based on observations Henry David Thoreau made during three walking tours of the Cape he undertook between 1849 and 1855. It illustrates the linkage of natural and social environments in terms of the class tensions associated with Irish immigration to New England. It presents arguments within a theory of ecocriticism. It also examines Thoreau's depiction of a Cohaset,

---

[1] Miller T K, Gallinat A S, Smith L C, Primack R B. "Comparing Fruiting Phenology across Two Historical Datasets: Thoreau's Observations and Herbarium Specimens". Annals of Botany, 2021, 128(2): 159–170.

[2] Fullerton T. "A Year at Play in the Woods of Walden Pond". Art Journal, 2020, 79(2): 95–104.

[3] Higgins R. "A Transcendentalist at Work". The American Scholar, 2020, 89(1): 71–76.

Massachusetts, shipwreck of a famine ship, drawing a connection between the Atlantic Ocean's natural border and class boundaries faced by Irish immigrants.[①]

Charles Yaple, in "Thoreau's Legacy Revisited", focuses on Henry David Thoreau's ideas of the relationship between human beings and the nature. It talks about the possible contributions of Thoreau on how outdoor educators can help deal with nature deficit disorder (NDD). Also discussed are ways on how outdoor educators can help children connect with the environment.[②]

Daniel J. Philippon, in "Thoreau's Notes on the 'Journey West': Nature Writing or Environmental History?", reconsiders the purpose, context and content of author Henry David Thoreau's notes about his trip to Minnesota and explores the significant challenges they pose for the contemporary reader. The primary reason for Thoreau's trip was to improve his failing health. His interest in Minnesota was tied not only to all the West symbolized, but also to all the West contained, including American Indians, frontier settlers and the region's indigenous flora and fauna. The abundance of botanical information contained in his notes as well as their piecemeal quality make it difficult to classify the writing as nonfiction nature writing or environmental history. This essay seeks to reclaim what has been seen by critics as weak or unimportant in these travel notes by revisioning the notes both a part of the emerging "literature of place" and as a bridge between the fields of environmental literature, history and ethics.[③]

Alan D. Hodder, in "The Gospel according to This Moment: Thoreau, Wildness, and American Nature Religion", suggests that "Ever since the Sierra Club adopted the slogan, 'In wildness is the preservation of the world', the text from which it was drawn—Thoreau's 1862 essay *Walking*—has been construed as a tribute to wild places. To some extent, this reading keeps faith with sentiments expressed in the essay. At the same time, a closer look suggests that the essay as a whole is really more about the life of the spirit than life in the wild. Despite the popular appropriation of *Walking* as a manifesto of environmentalist advocacy, some critics have questioned the usual view of *Walking*. Such observations also have a bearing on Thoreau's legacy as a progenitor of the literary expression of American nature spirituality. The purpose of this essay is to elucidate a particular experiential orientation to this spiritually-inflected notion of wildness, beginning with Thoreau and extending into the work of three literary exemplars of American nature religion—John Muir, Edward Abbey, and Annie Dillard".[④]

---

① Schneider R. "Drowning the Irish: Natural Borders and Class Boundaries in Henry David Thoreau's *Cape Cod*". American Transcendental Quarterly, 2008, 22(3): 463-476.

② Yaple C. "Thoreau's Legacy Revisited". Taproot Journal, 2005, 15(2): 10-13.

③ Philippon D J. "Thoreau's Notes on the 'Journey West': Nature Writing or Environmental History?". American Transcendental Quarterly, 2004, 18(2): 105-117.

④ Hodder A D. "The Gospel according to This Moment: Thoreau, Wildness, and American Nature Religion". Religion and the Arts, 2011, 15(4): 460-485.

2. Philosophical Study

Robert D. Richardson, in "Walden's Ripple Effect", discusses how author Henry David Thoreau lived on Walden Pond in Massachusetts for two years, in order to learn more about Thoreau's life. Topics discussed include publication of *Walden*, by Thoreau; analysis of the book; description of Thoreau's "habit of attention" for observing things around him; thoughts on Thoreau's philosophy; achievements that Thoreau was able to accomplish; and usefulness of the book as a practical manual on how to lead a good, just life.[①]

Christian Becker, in "Thoreau's Economic Philosophy", provides an encompassing portrayal of Thoreau's economic thought. "It is analyzed against the background of the history of economic thought and the economic thinking of his time. Thoreau's economic thought is an extensive examination of the ideas of classical political economy, and particularly of Jean-Baptiste Say, and it is a fundamental critique thereof. Thoreau recognizes that some aspects and foundations of the modern conception of the economy lead to an alienation of the human being from itself as well as to an alienation from nature. I demonstrate that this critique is a result of Thoreau's specific approach to the economy, which, based on his particular understanding of the human being and his philosophy of nature, seeks the meaning of the economy for human life and for nature. In this philosophical approach, which I characterize as an economic philosophy, Thoreau's deeper defiance of classical political economy and his original place within the history of economic thought are grounded. It leads Thoreau to an alternative conception of an economy of moderation, which is identified and described in detail. I conclude with considerations on the potential meaning of Thoreau's thought for current economic research".[②]

H. Berrezoug, in "Wilderness Ethics: Henry David Thoreau's Romantic Passion", "highlights the importance of wilderness in the American mind. Although wilderness had long been viewed as an ungodly place, transcendentalist American literature proved the opposite. Thus, this article proposes to discuss the way Henry David Thoreau' works, particularly *Walking* (1862), could foster new attitudes towards wilderness. In addition to the analysis of the symbolic and aesthetic dimensions of wilderness in Thoreau' works, this discussion seeks to measure the ecological dimensions of his works by highlighting his passion for preserving wilderness".[③]

Ira Brooker, in "Giving the Game away: Thoreau's Intellectual Imperialism and the Marketing of Walden Pond", suggests that the juxtaposition of Henry David Thoreau as the

---

① Richardson R D. "Walden's Ripple Effect". Smithsonian, 2004, 35(5): 106-111.
② Becker C. "Thoreau's Economic Philosophy". The European Journal of the History of Economic Thought, 2008, 15(2): 211-246.
③ Berrezoug H. "Wilderness Ethics: Henry David Thoreau's Romantic Passion". Al-Tawasul, 2015(43): 305-312.

Apostle of Unspoiled Nature against the sport utility vehicle crowd of marauders galumphing through forest, pond and prairie in search of new pleasures, may not be warranted. Thoreau, Brooker proposes, bears an ample measure of blame for marketing the wilderness and so of its despoliation. Topics discussed include misconception about Thoreau's ideas of balance of power between man and nature; review of related essays; and influences to the development of the Walden philosophy.[1]

Alan Fox, in "Guarding What Is Essential: Critiques of Material Culture in Thoreau and Yang Zhu", examines the comparison of the concept of natural destiny based on the philosophies of Henry David Thoreau and Yang Zhu. According to the author, Thoreau and Yang Zhu used similar social and cultural situations to emphasize the production, metabolism and retention of life force. It is inferred that these philosophers associated the efficient conservation of life force within the fulfillment of natural destiny, and both conformed to the conventional moralities and standards of success.[2]

Carl L. Bankston Lii, in "Thoreau's Case for Political Disengagement", discusses the views on government of 19th-century U.S. author Henry David Thoreau in his essay known as *Civil Disobedience*, published in 1849. The work is seen not as a call to political or social action, but as a statement of individual autonomy and political disengagement. Thoreau's refusal to pay a poll tax because of the U.S. involvement in the Mexican War and because of the legality of slavery is discussed. His acceptance of a jail sentence because of his nonpayment is also discussed. Subsequent interpretations of Thoreau's message are then evaluated.[3]

Jason P. Matzke, in "The John Brown Way: Frederick Douglass and Henry David Thoreau on the Use of Violence", discusses views of Frederick Douglass, a revolutionary author of Maryland, and Henry David Thoreau, an American essayist, poet, and practical philosopher, on the use of violence. The article makes specific reference to the use of violence by John Brown, a Northern white with a passionate hatred for chattel slavery, against slavery in his failed attempt on the federal arsenal at Harpers Ferry, Virginia, in 1859. The article views that Douglass's argument supporting Brown's use of violence is superior to Thoreau's.[4]

Yoshiaki Furui, in "Networked Solitude: *Walden*, or Life in Modern Communications", presents a critical discussion regarding the relationship of nineteenth-century U.S. poet and philosopher Henry David Thoreau with modernity. It also compares Thoreau with sixteenth-

---

[1] Brooker I. "Giving the Game away: Thoreau's Intellectual Imperialism and the Marketing of Walden Pond". The Midwest Quarterly, 2004, 45(2): 137-154.

[2] Fox A. "Guarding What Is Essential: Critiques of Material Culture in Thoreau and Yang Zhu". Philosophy East and West, 2008, 58(3): 358-371.

[3] Bankston Lii C L. "Thoreau's Case for Political Disengagement". Modern Age, 2010, 52(1): 6-13.

[4] Matzke J P. "The John Brown Way: Frederick Douglass and Henry David Thoreau on the Use of Violence". Massachusetts Review, 2005, 46(1): 62-75.

century French thinker Michel de Montaigne in terms of their views on solitude. The author discusses the kind of value Thoreau attached to the concept of solitude in spite of the myth of his self-reliance and individualism.①

Scott L. Pratt, in "Lessons in Place: Thoreau and Indigenous Philosophy", presents that "Some have argued that Indigenous and European Americans learned much from each other along the border. This paper examines the fate of the influence of Indigenous philosophy by considering the work of Henry David Thoreau. First, it summarizes the argument of *Native Pragmatism: Rethinking the Roots of American Philosophy* about the influence of Indigenous thought on American philosophy. In the second section, it discusses American philosophies of resistance in relation to the process of colonization. In the third section, it considers the later work of Thoreau as an example of the declining influence of Native thought on nineteenth-century American philosophy. On one hand, Thoreau adopted a philosophy of place that seems to emerge directly from his experiences with Indigenous Americans. On the other, he overtly sets aside the Indigenous conception of relational agency in favor of a Romantic conception of individuals over against both nature and civilization".②

Ryan Harper, in "Henry David Thoreau: A Man of Solitude Seeking Connection", looks at the work of U.S. philosopher Henry David Thoreau. A particular focus is given to Thoreau's essays, in which he made prophetic calling to fully awake watchers of Hebrew Scripture. The philosopher's ideas about individualism is discussed, particularly an individual's connections to people, places and processes.③

3. Post-colonial Study

Alex Moskowitz, in "Apathy, Political Emotion, and the Politics of Space in Thoreau's Antislavery Writing", takes "Thoreau's frustrations with the impossibility of perceiving the injustice of slavery as an invitation to discern within his larger corpus a distinct body of work that we can call Thoreau's antislavery writing. Beyond the mere topic of antislavery, I argue in this essay that Thoreau's antislavery writing is defined by a spatial politics that intersects with the politics of emotion: I argue that Thoreau is deeply invested in how the issue of slavery is consistently displaced spatially and emotionally". Through careful and close readings of a number of shorter entries from Thoreau's *Journal* and his major antislavery essays—including

---

① Furui Y. "Networked Solitude: *Walden*, or Life in Modern Communications". Texas Studies in Literature and Language, 2016, 58(3): 329-351.
② Pratt S L. "Lessons in Place: Thoreau and Indigenous Philosophy". Metaphilosophy, 2022, 53(4): 371-384.
③ Harper R. "Henry David Thoreau: A Man of Solitude Seeking Connection". America Magazine: The Jesuit Review of Faith & Culture, 2017(3): 38-43.

Civil Disobedience, *Slavery in Massachusetts*, *A Plea for Captain John Brown*, and *The Last Days of John Brown*—"I show how Thoreau returns throughout his career to a recurring set of images and rhetorical tropes to help conceptualize the immediate importance of abolition, even to those who think themselves too far removed from slavery to do anything about it, or to care. In his writing, Thoreau wants to know why slavery and the abolitionist cause engender such an apathetic response, and why, similarly, slavery appears to be such a distant issue. As I show, the emotional and spatial distance from the issue of slavery that Thoreau notes in his neighbors results from how economics compartmentalizes the political sphere. Political economy and the language of economics make the most pressing political issues always seem remote and insignificant. Thoreau is interested in how political conviction and action can become disjointed: just because you know something is wrong does not mean you are going to do anything about it. This essay, then, starts from a place of frustration. It tracks Thoreau's frustrations, and it pairs those frustrations with a shared set of politically coded images and rhetorical tropes to consider Thoreau not just as an antislavery speaker and figure, but also as a literary writer whose most complex thinking reveals itself to us when we treat him and his writing as such". [1]

4. Religious Study

Jake Halpern, in "Jungle Boy", describes his disillusionment with Henry David Thoreau's *Walden* after meeting a real hermit on vacation on Kauai (Hawaii). The hermit is named Donald. He lives in a paradisiacal wilderness, but he still has to deal with dirt, bodily functions and loneliness. The author suspects that Thoreau did not enjoy his time in the woods nearly as much as he claimed to. [2]

Alan D. Hodder, in "In the Nick of Time: Thoreau's 'Present' Experiment as a Colloquy of East and West", notes that "A central expression of the thematic structure of Henry David Thoreau's first two books, *A Week on the Concord and Merrimack Rivers* and *Walden*, and essential to several of the epiphanies that famously appear there, are his meditations on the nature and significance of time. Seldom, however, have these richly conceived passages been considered other than through strictly literary eyes. The objective of this essay is to examine the theological implications of Thoreau's representations of time with particular reference to two classical treatments that seem of particular relevance here: those found in Augustine's *Confessions* and the Hindu classic, the Bhagavad Gita. The purpose of this discussion is two-fold: to consider the theological cogency of Thoreau's treatment of time for its own sake and to

---

[1] Moskowitz A. "Apathy, Political Emotion, and the Politics of Space in Thoreau's Antislavery Writing". Criticism, 2022, 64(2): 139-160.
[2] Halpern J. "Jungle Boy". The New Republic, 2006, 235(1): 38.

reconsider Thoreau's position with respect to two theological traditions of which he was arguably an heir".[1]

James Dougherty, in "House-Building and House-Holding at Walden", discusses the content of the book *Walden* by Henry David Thoreau in relation to the construction of his own house at Walden Pond in Concord, Massachusetts. It explores Thoreau's phrasing in the book which gives precedence to the house, forming with the pond not a magic circle at Walden Pond, but an ellipse, double-centered. It highlights Thoreau's descriptions of an outward and sensible world that convey an inward and spiritual life, not imposed upon things and actions but discovered within them. In his book, Thoreau also resorted to the Christian idea of sacrament to describe those double-sided facts when they arose not from nature but from human practice.[2]

Jonathan Malesic, in "Henry David Thoreau's Anti-Work Spirituality and a New Theological Ethic of Work", suggests that although Henry David Thoreau stands outside the Christian canon, his outlook on the relations among spirituality, ecology, and economy highlights how Christian theologians can develop a theological work ethic in our era of economic and ecological precarity. He can furthermore help theologians counter the pro-work bias in much Christian thought. In *Walden*, Thoreau shows that the best work is an ascetic practice that reveals and reaps the abundance of nature and connects the person to the immanent divine and thereby glimpsing eternity. Thoreau thus offers the outline of a transformed theology of work even as he challenges Protestant vocationalism in the early industrial era. He is therefore a fitting if challenging guide for formulating a theology of the self as agent and product of work, at a moment when the postindustrial ideal of work that is both meaningful and remunerative seems ever more unattainable while the negative impact of our work on nonhuman nature is ever more apparent.[3]

Erin McCoy, in "Civil Disobedience under God: Breaking Binaries of Antiwar Protest and Faith", presents a literary criticism of the essay *Civil Disobedience*, by Henry David Thoreau. It analyzes the language and the approach of the author, focusing on the reason behind the conscience of a man. It also mentions about the nonviolent protest discussed in the essay that links the acts of civil disobedience with religious beliefs.[4]

J. Heath Atchley, in "Sounding the Depth of the Secular: Tillich with Thoreau", articulates a version of the concept of depth that is socially critical by examining some of the thought of Paul Tillich and Henry David Thoreau. For both thinkers, depth is a concept that works to disrupt the

---

[1] Hodder A D. "In the Nick of Time: Thoreau's 'Present' Experiment as a Colloquy of East and West". Religion and the Arts, 2005, 9(3): 235-257.

[2] Dougherty J. "House-Building and House-Holding at Walden". Christianity and Literature, 2008, 57(2): 224-250.

[3] Malesic J. "Henry David Thoreau's Anti-Work Spirituality and a New Theological Ethic of Work". The Journal of Religious Ethics, 2017, 45(2): 309-329.

[4] McCoy E. "Civil Disobedience under God: Breaking Binaries of Antiwar Protest and Faith". Interdisciplinary Humanities, 2016, 33(2): 65-72.

rigid division between the secular and the religious. Such criticism, of a structure so fundamental to modern experience, suggests that the concept of depth is not simply a mystifying supporter of established power. Instead, it can play an important role in a religious, yet progressive, critical social thought.①

Scott Morrison, in "To Be a Believer in Republican Turkey: Three Allegories of İsmet Özel", focuses on the Islamist works of Turkish Islamist intellectual İsmet Özel. In his extended autobiographical essay *Waldo Sen Neden Burada Değilsin?* (*Why Aren't You Here Waldo?*), Özel places a response to Henry David Thoreau, who was at the time incarcerated for protesting against the Mexican-American war. Özel's portrayal of the exchange, and the association of his own life with Thoreau's, accentuate two pervasive characteristics of a new type of Muslim writer and writing emerging in Turkey since the late 1970s. His treatises and topics overlap with the works of Turkish Islamists of his same generation.②

5. Ethical Study

Rick Anthony Furtak, in "Thoreau's Emotional Stoicism", focuses on the indications of author Henry David Thoreau's emotional stoicism. Topics discussed include Thoreau's notion that being a philosopher is not merely a matter of theory but more importantly of practice; Thoreau's tendency to speak as if knowledge is consummated in tranquility; and Thoreau's deep agreement with the Stoic idea that, while most of us live in an antlike state of petty agitation, it is within our power to liberate ourselves from the belief that trivial and superfluous objects are essential to our well-being.③

Alda Balthrop-Lewis, in "Exemplarist Environmental Ethics: Thoreau's Political Asceticism against Solution Thinking", argues that "environmental ethics can deemphasize environmental problem-solving in preference for a more exemplarist mode. This mode will renarrate what we admire in those we have long admired, in order to make them resonate with contemporary ethical needs. First, I outline a method problem that arose for me in ethnographic fieldwork, a problem that I call, far too reductively, 'solution thinking'. Second, I relate that method problem to movements against 'quandary ethics' in ethical theory more broadly. Third, I discuss some interpretive work I am engaged in about Henry David Thoreau and how it bears on the methodological issues my fieldwork raised. I argue that some of the most important icons of right relation to environment, especially Francis of Assisi and Thoreau, should be envisioned as far

---

① Atchley J H. "Sounding the Depth of the Secular: Tillich with Thoreau". Implicit Religion, 2012, 15(2): 153-166.
② Morrison S. "To Be a Believer in Republican Turkey: Three Allegories of İsmet Özel". The Muslim World, 2006, 96(3): 507-521.
③ Furtak R A. "Thoreau's Emotional Stoicism". The Journal of Speculative Philosophy, 2003, 17(2): 122-132.

more politically invested than they usually are. They demonstrate to scholars of religious ethics that an exemplarist ethic focused on character need not neglect politics".[1]

Lee A. Mcbride Lii, in "Insurrectionist Ethics and Thoreau", examines philosopher Leonard Harris' concept of insurrectionist ethics, which supports human liberation from oppression through revolution, as it applies to the thought of philosopher Henry David Thoreau. The author does this as a means to complicate the traditional understanding of American philosophy as entirely concerned with the peaceful expansion of democracy and liberalism. Consideration is given to four features of insurrectionist ethics that can be identified in Thoreau: the defying of the authority and suasionist rhetoric of the U.S. government, a belief in moral action against brutality, the use of representative heuristics in his discussion of African American slavery, and support for such character traits as audacity and irreverence.[2]

6. Canonization Study

Tatiana Venediktova, in "Communication 'in the Higher Sense': Young Thoreau and Young Dostoyevski", discusses the art of conversation as a particular configuration of intersubjectivity and the corresponding technique of communication based on the works of Henry David Thoreau and Fyodor Dostoyevski. Topics discussed include analysis of the books published by the authors; information on how Thoreau interacts with nature; and role of nature in teaching humans how to communicate.[3]

Jeffrey Utzinger, in "Henry David Thoreau's Slumbering Capability: Envisioning John Brown as Carlylean Hero", explores the influence of author Thomas Carlyle on author Henry David Thoreau in regards to the concept of heroism and the violent tactics of anti-slavery activist John Brown. Emphasis is given to topics such as nonviolence in the abolitionist movement, the book *On Heroes, Hero-Worship, and the Heroic in History*, and Thoreau's depiction of Brown as a hero and martyr.[4]

7. New Historicism Study

Richard Prud'Homme, in "*Walden*'s Economy of Living", presents information on the

---

[1] Balthrop-Lewis A. "Exemplarist Environmental Ethics: Thoreau's Political Ascetism against Solution Thinking". The Journal of Religious Ethics, 2019, 47(3): 525-550.
[2] Mcbride Lii L A. "Insurrectionist Ethics and Thoreau". Transactions of the Charles S. Peirce Society, 2013, 49(1): 29-45.
[3] Venediktova T. "Communication 'in the Higher Sense': Young Thoreau and Young Dostoyevski". American Studies International, 2003, 41(1/2): 140-151.
[4] Utzinger J. "Henry David Thoreau's Slumbering Capability: Envisioning John Brown as Carlylean Hero". The Midwest Quarterly, 2015, 56(2): 186-202.

book *Walden*, by Henry David Thoreau. *Walden* discusses the concept of political economy. The author of this essay argues that Thoreau's "economy of living" is acutely economics as no disciple of the Thoreauvian simple life would be willing to concede. Topics discussed include historical background of the economic condition of the United States; views on the business and economy cycles; details on the concept of naturalism; and discussion on the autobiographical content of the book.[①]

Randall Conrad, in "'I Heard a Very Loud Sound': Thoreau Processes the Spectacle of Sudden, Violent Death", examines Henry David Thoreau's narratives in relation to several related journal entries during 1853, as well as related lectures, essays and correspondence by Thoreau around this time. Thoreau was, in fact, a professional when it came to the powder-milling industry. Apart from the need for safety precautions, milling gunpowder is akin to milling graphite. Thoreau's journal presents internal clues that invite a more complex interpretation of its narrative voice. "Thoreau's account of the disaster occurs, like the explosion itself, is a disruption of broader and more peaceful reflections on nature and the seasons' cycle which comprise the overall entry for the day". "Thoreau's biographers agree that he was in a generally grim mood during this winter of 1853. Sensitive to the approach of midlife, Thoreau saw mortality everywhere, a state strongly reinforced by the spectacle at the molls".[②]

Patrick Lacroix, in "Finding Thoreau in French Canada: The Ideological Legacy of the American Revolution", suggests that "Henry David Thoreau's *A Yankee in Canada* is easily overlooked. Because it is so selective in its depiction of life in the St. Lawrence River valley, historians of mid-nineteenth-century Canada have shown little interest in Thoreau's first-hand account. To American readers, it offers little of the characteristic Thoreau found in *Walden* and *Resistance to Civil Government*. Yet, it is highly significant as an expression of national self-definition. Thoreau borrowed themes at least as old as the American Revolution when noting the pernicious rule of Catholic and British power in Canada. He set out to expose the promise of republican values by emphasizing the contrast between these and the poor and morally stunted life under Old World institutions. His work must therefore be interpreted as a call to his audience to commit more deeply than ever to the ideals that animated the Great Republic's founding moment. It must also stand as a civic interpretation of American nationality at a time when this perspective was waning. Before long, Old World peoples would be racialized and the ideological embrace of the republican values advanced by Thoreau would no longer suffice in making American citizens".[③]

---

① Prud'Homme R. "*Walden*'s Economy of Living". Raritan, 2001, 20(3): 107-131.
② Conrad R. "'I Heard a Very Loud Sound': Thoreau Processes the Spectacle of Sudden, Violent Death". American Transcendental Quarterly, 2005, 19(2): 81-94.
③ Lacroix P. "Finding Thoreau in French Canada: The Ideological Legacy of the American Revolution". American Review of Canadian Studies, 2017, 47(3): 266-279.

Robert A. Gross, in "Thoreau and the Laborers of Concord", presents a literary criticism about the book *Walden*. Particular focus is given to the book's depiction of laborers in 19th century Concord, Massachusetts, including Irish laborers and farmers. An overview of Thoreau's perspective on land ownership, as portrayed in *Walden*, is provided.[1]

Fernando J. Rodríguez, in "The Outcast, the Expatriate and the Outlaw; Thoreau, Pound and Thompson's America", discusses the association between American authors and outlaws, tricksters, expatriates and outcasts from the mid-19th century through the early 2000s. Particular focus is given to examining the lives and literature of the American writers Henry David Thoreau, Ezra Pound and Hunter S. Thompson.[2]

Timothy Sweet, in "Projecting Early American Environmental Writing", explores early American environmental writing and the role that author Henry David Thoreau played in the creation of an American environmental literary periodization. It examines the changes that Thoreau brought to environmental writing, explores colonial-period environmental writing, and discusses the difference between literature that examined the revitalizing powers of nature and literature that examined the human connection to nature through labor and production.[3]

8. Thematic Study

Luke Philip Plotica, in "Singing Oneself or Living Deliberately: Whitman and Thoreau on Individuality and Democracy", suggests that "The individual stands at the center of the works of Walt Whitman and Henry David Thoreau. Prompted to their reflections by the changing social, economic, and political conditions of nineteenth century America, they articulate two rich and distinct visions of individuality and the conditions that foster and frustrate its development. Whitman's poetry and prose depicts a porous, malleable, internally plural self who experiences the world in largely aesthetic terms and ecstatic terms, whereas Thoreau's writings depict a bounded, willful self who experiences the world through the mediating force of her individual ethical principles. Thus, while both valorized individuality, they present competing ideals: Whitman's was expansive and centrifugal, while Thoreau's was integral and centripetal. Furthermore, their respective accounts of democracy—the former's laudatory, the latter's critical—are profoundly shaped by these antecedent accounts of the individual. In this

---

[1] Gross R A. "Thoreau and the Laborers of Concord". Raritan, 2013, 33(1): 50-66.
[2] Rodríguez F J. "The Outcast, the Expatriate and the Outlaw; Thoreau, Pound and Thompson's America". Atenea, 2012, 32(1/2): 31-48.
[3] Sweet T. "Projecting Early American Environmental Writing". American Literay History, 2010, 22(2): 419-431.

essay, I argue that not only do these distinct visions of individuality continue to speak to us today, they stand to inform analysis of and attachment to modern democratic institutions and practices".①

9. Bibliographical Study

Danny Heitman, in "Not Exactly a Hermit: Henry David Thoreau", discusses the life and career of the American author Henry David Thoreau. The author pays particular attention to Thoreau's reputation as a loner and hermit. The author of this article notes that "Henry David Thoreau went in for society, but on his own terms". Other topics addressed include Thoreau's book *Walden*, his correspondence, and his writing style. Comments by Elizabeth Witherell, editor-in-chief of *The Writings of Henry D. Thoreau*, are included.②

Laurie Champion, in "'I Keep Looking Back to See Where I've Been': Bobbie Ann Mason's *Clear Springs* and Henry David Thoreau's *Walden*", discusses the depiction of human growth and maturity in Bobbie Ann Mason's memoir *Clear Springs* and Henry David Thoreau's *Walden*. Topics discussed include outline of the seasons followed in the memoir; reason behind the emphasis placed on the conflict between leaving and staying home in *Clear Springs*; and use of metaphors of geography by Thoreau to explain how spiritual growth is achieved.③

Markus Poetzsch, in "Sounding Walden Pond: The Depths and 'Double Shadows' of Thoreau's Autobiographical Symbol", examines the autobiographical symbol of the pond in Henry David Thoreau's *Walden*. According to the author, most studies that explored the pond's symbolism tend to consider it as a distillation of the quest narrative or pilgrimage. It becomes a locus and reflection of spiritual rebirth and ethical reform. One example is Melvin Lyon's study wherein his discussion of the pond focused on the moral attributes of depth and purity. He argued that for Thoreau, the pond is both a standard by which he can measure his improvement, as well as an influence upon his progress. This only shows that the pond serves as a guide or prophet.④

---

① Plotica L P. "Singing Oneself or Living Deliberately: Whitman and Thoreau on Individuality and Democracy". Transactions of the Charles S. Peirce Society, 2017, 53(4): 601-621.

② Heitman D. "Not Exactly a Hermit: Henry David Thoreau". Humanities, 2012, 33(5): 14-50.

③ Champion L. "'I Keep Looking Back to See Where I've Been': Bobbie Ann Mason's *Clear Springs* and Henry David Thoreau's *Walden*". The Southern Literary Journal, 2004, 36(2): 47-58.

④ Poetzsch M. "Sounding Walden Pond: The Depths and 'Double Shadows' of Thoreau's Autobiographical Symbol". American Transcendental Quarterly, 2008, 22(2): 387-401.

10. Psychological Study

Kent Bicknell, in "Brooks and Ditches: A Transcendental Look at Education", presents an analysis of Transcendentalist Henry David Thoreau's statement about ditches and brooks which he relates to education. Education was of great interest to Transcendentalists and they were stimulated by the dynamic of how to best incorporate the individual and the society and how to create the ideal grounds. They consider each child as a meandering brook, sacred and free by nature, rather than a raw resource to be converted to a straight-cut ditch for societal ends.[1]

Geoff Wisner, in "At the Doorway of Solitude: Even Henry David Thoreau Knew that One Could Be Too Alone", discusses the role of solitude in success of essayist, poet, and philosopher Henry David Thoreau. Topics discussed include the role of solitude to understand simplicity and self-reliance; importance of solitude for personal development; and information on Thoreau's essay *Resistance to Civil Government* which attempt to prevent the Seabrook nuclear power plant from being built.[2]

Forough Barani, and Wan Roselezam Wan Yahya, in "Literary Art as a Form of Self-Inquiry in Thoreau's *Walden*", suggest that "In his non-fiction work *Walden*, Henry David Thoreau's internal dialogues and meditations reveal to us his 'self' as embodied in his literary work. While in this selected work, there is a close analogy between self and the text, which both are a series of inner voices juxtaposed with and often contradicting one another, in order to decipher the artist's persona, this study frames its analysis within two perspectives: the sociolinguistics (Bakhtin's 'Dialogism') and psychology (Herman's 'Dialogical Self'). This attempt to investigate the aesthetic and ideological statements of the narrator of *Walden* explores the extent of nature's influence on him as an alienated writer; and examines the cultural heritage in the context of American society of Thoreau to identify the roots of the broken ties between 'self' and the 'society' to shed light on the individual and social self of the narrator in *Walden*. This study concludes that this selected non-fiction work is not just a monological poetic meditation of its author, but a polyphonic contemplation of internal voices carnivalizing the social ideologies of its time embodied in his art as a pursuit of self inquiry".[3]

---

[1] Bicknell K. "Brooks and Ditches: A Transcendental Look at Education". Independent School, 2008, 68(1): 82–88.

[2] Wisner G. "At the Doorway of Solitude: Even Henry David Thoreau Knew that One Could Be Too Alone". Phi Kappa Phi Forum, 2021, 101(1): 22–23.

[3] Barani F, Wan Yahya W R. "Literary Art as a Form of Self-Inquiry in Thoreau's *Walden*". International Journal of Interdisciplinary Social Sciences, 2010, 5(1): 39–51.

11. Aesthetics Study

John Charles Ryan, in "Sense of Place and Sense of Taste: Thoreau's Botanical Aesthetics", focuses on the botanical works of philosopher Henry David Thoreau and the aesthetics of nature. Topics discussed include Thoreau's botanical writing, such as *The Dispersion of Seeds* and *Wild Seeds*. These essays contain some details about the distribution, shape and size of fruits combined with aesthetic, and Thoreau's subjective observations. "As a transdisciplinarian, Thoreau's fascination for the local environment of Concord was not only scientific, but also cultural, historical, and spiritual". "As many contemporary environmental writers have underscored, ecology is the study of the earth 'household'. At the heart of Thoreau's protoecological writings is an aesthetics of the natural world. His ecological aesthetics resists paradigms of beauty that privilege art over nature, humanity over nonhuman life, and vision over the non-ocular senses of sound, taste, touch, smell, and spatial orientation. Moreover, Thoreau's aesthetic approach to ecology and the natural world is an embodied—rather than visually distanced—one".[①]

Sean Ross Meeham, in "Pencil of Nature: Thoreau's Photographic Register", presents a critical investigation on the register of photography in the works of writer Henry David Thoreau. The author explores the juxtaposition of photography and writing in Thoreau's work. He argues that Thoreau engages the new visual technology of representation as a crucial figure for his writing. This article illustrates the own interest of Thoreau in photography and the complex use of its language in his writing. The author states that the photographic register of Thoreau calls the attention of the readers to a technological concept of graphic reproduction.[②]

12. Post-colonial Study

James J. Donahue, in "'Hardly the Voice of the Same Man': *Civil Disobedience* and Thoreau's Response to John Brown", presents a look at the essay *Civil Disobedience* by Henry David Thoreau. The social and political circumstances of Thoreau's era are described, including slavery and abolition movements. Also presented is a discussion of Thoreau's response to the

---

① Ryan J C. "Sense of Place and Sense of Taste: Thoreau's Botanical Aesthetics". Interdisciplinary Humanities, 2015, 32(3): 63-78.
② Meeham S R. "Pencil of Nature: Thoreau's Photographic Register". Criticism, 2006, 48(1): 7-38.

abolitionist John Brown, who led a raid on the Harpers Ferry Armory, in his essays *A Plea for Captain John Brown* and *The Last Days of John Brown*.[①]

13. Special Study

John S. Pipkin, in "Hiding Places: Thoreau's Geographies", presents that "For Henry David Thoreau, penetrating landscape observation provided an unfailing point of departure for natural description, ecstatic contemplation, and violently paradoxical social commentary. His texts express, question, naturalize, and deploy many presuppositions about geographic order in the landscape. His writing life, ending in 1862, spanned a time when teleological explanations of the landscape were challenged by the gradual 'detheologization' of scientific thought. The new views on the ultimate geographic role of Providence all made some room for empirical, proximate explanations of geography's grand theme: the fit between humanity and the earth. The effect of Thoreau's development from transcendental idealism to a penetrating yet fussy empiricism was to dissolve the unity of the human and natural worlds. His odd, shifting, rhetorical appropriation of place, his resistance to unqualified generalization, and his purported aversion to travel (outside of Concord) all contrast with the path geography took during the second—Darwinian—half of the century. Because he was well informed about the science of his time and about Humboldt and Guyot in particular, and because his texts are rich literary contrivances, geographers may fruitfully examine his work in two ways: first, as a register of educated thought about landscape before geography's modern institutionalization as a discipline, and second, as a complex of written landscapes, inscribing and erasing places in varied ways, expressing the contradictions of early modernism".[②]

W. Barksdale Maynard, in "Thoreau's House at Walden", examines the little frame house which Henry David Thoreau constructed for himself at Walden Pond in Concord, Massachusetts in 1845. Topics discussed include description of Thoreau's lakeshore experiment viewed in the context of contemporary architectural thought; details on Thoreau's architecture; picturesque influences in siting house and garden; and information on Thoreau's book *Walden*.[③]

---

① Donahue J J. "'Hardly the Voice of the Same Man': *Civil Disobedience* and Thoreau's Response to John Brown". The Midwest Quarterly, 2007, 48(2): 247-265.
② Pipkin J S. "Hiding Places: Thoreau's Geographies". Annals of the Association of American Geographers, 2001, 91(3): 527-545.
③ Maynard W B. "Thoreau's House at Walden". Art Bulletin,1999, 81(2): 303325.

14. Feminism Study

Michael Warner, in "Thoreau's Bottom", looks at Henry David Thoreau's views on sexuality and gender identity as seen from the entries he made in a journal he kept while living in Walden. Topics discussed include challenge to the notion that sexual desire derives from the mere fact of gender difference; longing for self-transcendence through the love of another man; and Thoreau as a representation of self-reflexive desire.[①]

15. Cultural Study

Iuliu Rațiu, in "Surveying the Interval: Henry David Thoreau's Climb of Saddle-back Mountain in *A Week on the Concord and Merrimack Rivers*", presents that "In July 1844, on route to the Catskill Mountains in New York, Henry David Thoreau climbed Saddleback Mt. (now Greylock), the highest natural point in Massachusetts. Situated in the northwestern part of the state, the mountain is traversed by a network of hiking trails, including the tail end of the Appalachian Trail. Thoreau later described this experience in his first published book *A Week on the Concord and Merrimack Rivers*, whose manuscript he wrote during his stay at Walden Pond between 1845 and 1847. In my paper, I analyze Thoreau's description of the climb and cast the ascent as a meditation in the Romantic tradition of the quest for the sacred and for the sublime".[②]

---

① Warner M. "Thoreau's Bottom". Raritan, 1992, 11(3): 53-78.
② Rațiu I. "Surveying the Interval: Henry David Thoreau's Climb of Saddle-back Mountain in *A Week on the Concord and Merrimack Rivers*". Bulletin of the Transilvania University of Brasov, Series IV: Philology & Cultural Studies, 2016, 9(1): 67-80.

Chapter 15
Mark Twain

Mark Twain (1835-1910)

Mark Twain was an American humorist, journalist, lecturer, and novelist who acquired international fame for his travel narratives, especially *The Innocents Abroad* (1869), *Roughing It* (1872), and *Life on the Mississippi* (1883), and for his adventure stories of boyhood, especially *The Adventures of Tom Sawyer* (1876) and *Adventures of Huckleberry Finn* (1884). As a gifted raconteur, distinctive humorist, and irascible moralist, he transcended the apparent limitations of his origins to become a popular public figure and one of America's best and most beloved writers.[1]

---

[1] https://www.britannica.com/biography/Mark-Twain.

Critical Perspectives

1. Thematic Study

Jarret S. Lovell, in "On Field Mice, Butterflies, and Tigers: Mark Twain's *Ten Commandments* and Circumstance-based Justice", offers the author's insights regarding the essay *Fables of Man* which focuses on the identities of two murderers. He mentions that Twain has used direct and clear language to illustrate criminal justice system. He argues that *The Ten Commandments* cannot alter the circumstance or temperament of animals while penal law can do less to tackle the economic, social and emotional circumstances of criminals.[1]

2. Cultural Study

Mark Storey, in "Huck and Hank Go to the Circus: Mark Twain under Barnum's Big Top", argues that Mark Twain's acquaintance with P. T. Barnum, and more especially Twain's fascination with the world of popular entertainment that Barnum epitomized, provided inspiration and material for some of Twain's most enduring works. In particular, the essay argues that two of Twain's most revered novels—*Adventures of Huckleberry Finn* (1884) and *A Connecticut Yankee at King Arthur's Court* (1889)—are invested both thematically and generically in the complex cultural associations of the postbellum circus. Embodying the commercial capitalism of industrialized America whilst also offering a romantic liberation from everyday life, the circus becomes a condensation of many of the competing impulses of Twain's life and work—between irreverent humour and sober social critique, and between the desire for imaginative freedom and a recognition of financial imperatives.[2]

---

[1] Lovell J S. "On Field Mice, Butterflies, and Tigers: Mark Twain's *Ten Commandments* and Circumstance-based Justice". Contemporary Justice Review, 2012, 15(2): 173–176.

[2] Storey M. "Huck and Hank Go to the Circus: Mark Twain under Barnum's Big Top". European Journal of American Culture, 2010, 29(3): 217–228.

3. Religious Study

Joe B. Fulton, in "Mark Twain's New Jerusalem: Prophecy in the Unpublished Essay 'About Cities in the Sun'", reflects on an unpublished essay of Mark Twain. It has remained unpublished for a century in Twain's possession. The delay in publication was due to the significant gap in scholarly understanding of Twain's relationship to the biblical genre of prophecy. Furthermore, the essay covers Twain's appropriation of prophecy as a literary genre.[1]

4. Narrative Study

Melissa Hart, in "Make 'em Laugh: Editors Want Short Humorous Essays That Both Entertain and Enlighten", discusses the factors to consider in writing short humorous essays. It highlights the work of Mark Twain, a writer who understood the universal appeal of humor and how to blend it smoothly into social and political commentary. Author Leigh Anne Jasheway-Bryant emphasizes that a good humorous essay appeals to both the body and the head. Kalle Lasn, editor of the activist journal *Adbusters*, notes that informative essays that rely on personal stories depict the trend toward such literary journalism.[2]

---

[1] Fulton J B. "Mark Twain's New Jerusalem: Prophecy in the Unpublished Essay 'About Cities in the Sun'". Christianity & Literature, 2006, 55(2): 173-194.

[2] Hart M. "Make' em Laugh: Editors Want Short Humorous Essays That Both Entertain and Enlighten". Writer (Kalmbach Publishing Co.), 2006, 119(3): 48-50.

Chapter 16
Elwyn Brooks White

Elwyn Brooks White (1899-1985)

  E. B. White was an American essayist, author, and literary stylist, whose eloquent, unaffected prose appealed to readers of all ages. White graduated from Cornell University in Ithaca, New York, in 1921 and worked as a reporter and freelance writer before joining *The New Yorker* magazine as a writer and contributing editor in 1927. He married Katherine Sergeant Angell, *The New Yorker*'s first fiction editor, in 1929, and he remained with the weekly magazine for the rest of his career. White's essays for *The New Yorker* quickly garnered critical praise. Written in a personal, direct style that showcased an affable sense of humour, his witty pieces contained musings about city life, politics, and literature, among other subjects. White also wrote poems, cartoon captions, and brief sketches for the magazine, and his writings helped establish its intellectual and cosmopolitan tone. White collaborated with James Thurber on *Is Sex Necessary?* (1929), a spoof of contemporary sex manuals. In a monthly column (1938–1943) for *Harper's Magazine*, he wrote essays about rural life.[1]

---

[1] https://www.britannica.com/biography/E-B-White.

Critical Perspectives

1. Narrative Study

Raymond A. Schroth, in "Two for the Road", presents information on travel writing, which is written by authors who have never been to the place. "The best travel writing is usually about something else—not just been-there and saw-that. There is an inner voyage, even for the atheist, a spiritual experience—if not an encounter with God at least a glimpse into the mystery of life embodied in crumbling walls or crashing waves." It is stated that the travels of E. B. White, the New York-based essayist and coauthor, with William Strunk, author of the book *The Elements of Style*, seldom took him far from his homes in Maine, Florida and New York.[1]

Betty Kelly Sargent, in "Three Books on Writing Well for Indie Authors", presents recommended books on writing for independent (indie) authors. The books discussed include *The Elements of Style* by William Strunk Jr. and E. B. White, *On Writing Well: The Classic Guide to Writing Nonfiction* by William Zinsser, and *Wired for Story: The Writer's Guide to Using Brain Science to Hook Readers from the Very First Sentence* by Lisa Cron.[2]

Geoff Pullum, in "The 'However' Myth", discusses the proper grammatical use of the adverb, and argues that recommendations from authors William Strunk Jr. and E. B. White regarding its linguistically correct form are outdated and incorrect. He comments on authors including Oscar Wilde who have used the term at the beginning of sentences, which Strunk and White state is incorrect, and discusses topics including standard English, grammar instruction, and ambiguity.[3]

2. Biographical Study

Danny Heitman, in "The White Pages", points out that "America's greatest personal essayist was more than a little shy and intensely self-conscious". This article discusses the writings done by author E. B. White while living at his farm in Maine. Topics discussed include *One Man's Meat*, a collection of essays published in the periodical *Harper's Magazine*; White's

---

[1] Schroth R A. "Two for the Road". America Magazine: The Jesuit Review of Faith & Culture, 2012, 206(3): 24-25.
[2] Sargent B K. "Three Books on Writing Well for Indie Authors". Publishers Weekly, 2014, 261(16): 36.
[3] Pullum G. "The 'However' Myth". The Chronicle of Higher Education, 2012(58): 2.

writing in publication *The New Yorker* in the years before he moved to his farm; and his children's book *Charlotte's Web*.①

3. New Historicism Study

Timothy P. Schilling, in "Rooftop Perspective", reflects on the stand of author E. B. White on the fight against terrorism, with reference to his book *One Man's Meat*. Topics discussed include excerpt from a passage he has written in the article *Salt Water Farm* which appeared in January 1939; purpose of terrorism; contribution of White in preserving peace as reflected in his 1949 essay *Spring*.②

Geoffrey K. Pullum, in "50 Years of Stupid Grammar Advice", discusses the book *The Elements of Style* by William Strunk Jr. and E. B. White. Despite the fact that the book is held in esteem by American college graduates, the author believes that it is largely worthless and has significantly degraded American students' grasp of English grammar. The author cites the book's treatment of the active voice and the passive voice as evidence that it is a poor resource for writers, pointing out the fact that many of its examples of passive constructions are incorrect.③

4. Biographical Study

Michael Sims, in "The Nature of E. B. White", presents a profile of children's author Elwyn Brooks White and examines how his childhood growing up on a family farm influenced his writing about the natural and animal world. This article chronicles how his witnessing a spider web being formed in his family's barn influenced his book *Charlotte's Web*, comments on critical views of White's use of anthropomorphism in his books *Stuart Little* and *The Trumpet of the Swan*, and discusses how White wrote letters to his wife Katharine S. White from the perspective of their Scottish terrier Daisy.④

---

① Heitman D. "The White Pages". Humanities, 2014, 35(1): 20–51.
② Schilling T P. "Rooftop Perspective". Commonweal, 2003, 130(19): 14–17.
③ Pullum G K. "50 Years of Stupid Grammar Advice". The Chronicle of Higher Education, 2009, 55(32): B15–B16.
④ Sims M. "The Nature of E. B. White". The Chronicle of Higher Education, 2011, 57(38): B17–B19.

Appendix

Of Studies

By Francis Bacon

Studies serve for delight, for ornament, and for ability. Their chief use for delight, is in privateness and retiring; for ornament, is in discourse; and for ability, is in the judgment and disposition of business. For expert men can execute, and perhaps judge of particulars, one by one; but the general counsels, and the plots and marshalling of affairs come best from those that are learned.

To spend too much time in studies is sloth; to use them too much for ornament is affection; to make judgment wholly by their rules is the humor of a scholar. They perfect nature and are perfected by experience: for natural abilities are like natural plants, that need pruning by study, and studies themselves do give forth directions too much at large, except they be bounded in by experience.

Crafty men contemn studies, simple men admire them, and wise men use them, for they teach not their own use; but that is a wisdom without them and above them, won by observation. Read not to contradict and confuse; nor to believe and take for granted; nor to find talk and discourse; but to weigh and consider.

Some books are to be tasted, others to be swallowed, and some few to be chewed and digested; that is, some books are to be read only in parts; others to be read, but not curiously; and some few to be ready wholly, and with diligence and attention. Some books also may be read by deputy and extracts made of them by others; but that would be only in the less important arguments, and the meaner sort of books; else distilled books are, like common distilled waters, flashy things.

  Reading makes a full man; conference a ready man; and writing an exact man. And therefore, if a man write little, he had need have a great memory; if he confer little, he had need have a present wit; and if he read little, he had need have much cunning, to seem to know that he doth not.

  Histories make men wise; poets witty; the mathematics subtle; natural philosophy deep; moral grave; logic and rhetoric able to contend. Abeunt studia in mores. Nay there is no stond or impediment in the wit, but may be wrought out by fit studies: like as diseases of the body may have appropriate exercises. Bowling is good for the stone and reins; shooting for the lungs and breast; gentle walking for the stomach; riding for the head; and the like. So if a man's wit be wandering, let him study the mathematics; for in demonstrations, if his wit be called away never so little, he must begin again. If his wit be not apt to distinguish or find differences, let him study the schoolmen; for they are cymini sectores. If he be not apt to beat over matters, and to call up one thing to prove and illustrate another, let him study the lawyers' cases. So every defect of the mind may have a special receipt.

A Treatise on Good Manners and Good Breeding

By Jonathan Swift

Good manners is the art of making those people easy with whom we converse.

Whoever makes the fewest persons uneasy is the best bred in the company.

As the best law is founded upon reason, so are the best manners. And as some lawyers have introduced unreasonable things into common law, so likewise many teachers have introduced absurd things into common good manners.

One principal point of this art is to suit our behaviour to the three several degrees of men; our superiors, our equals, and those below us.

For instance, to press either of the two former to eat or drink is a breach of manners; but a farmer or a tradesman must be thus treated, or else it will be difficult to persuade them that they are welcome.

Pride, ill nature, and want of sense, are the three great sources of ill manners; without some one of these defects, no man will behave himself ill for want of experience; or of what, in the language of fools, is called knowing the world.

I defy any one to assign an incident wherein reason will not direct us what we are to say or do in company, if we are not misled by pride or ill nature.

Therefore I insist that good sense is the principal foundation of good manners; but because the former is a gift which very few among mankind are possessed of, therefore all the civilized nations of the world have agreed upon fixing some rules for common behaviour, best suited to their general customs, or fancies, as a kind of artificial good sense, to supply the defects of reason. Without which the gentlemanly part of dunces would be perpetually at cuffs, as they seldom fail when they happen to be drunk, or engaged in squabbles about women or play. And, God be thanked, there hardly happens a duel in a year, which may not be imputed to one of those three motives. Upon which account, I should be exceedingly sorry to find the legislature make any new laws against the practice of duelling; because the methods are easy and many for a wise man to avoid a quarrel with honour, or engage in it with innocence. And I can discover no political evil in suffering bullies, sharpers, and rakes, to rid the world of each other by a method of their own; where the law hath not been able to find an expedient.

As the common forms of good manners were intended for regulating the conduct of those who have weak understandings; so they have been corrupted by the persons for whose use they were contrived. For these people have fallen into a needless and endless way of multiplying ceremonies, which have been extremely troublesome to those who practise them, and insupportable to everybody else: insomuch that wise men are often more uneasy at the over civility of these refiners, than they could possibly be in the conversations of peasants or mechanics.

The impertinencies of this ceremonial behaviour are nowhere better seen than at those tables where ladies preside, who value themselves upon account of their good breeding; where a man must reckon upon passing an hour without doing any one thing he has a mind to; unless he will be so hardy to break through all the settled decorum of the family. She determines what he loves best, and how much he shall eat; and if the master of the house happens to be of the same disposition, he proceeds in the same tyrannical manner to prescribe in the drinking part: at the same time, you are under the necessity of answering a thousand apologies for your entertainment. And although a good deal of this humour is pretty well worn off among many people of the best fashion, yet too much of it still remains, especially in the country; where an honest gentleman assured me, that having been kept four days, against his will, at a friend's house, with all the circumstances of hiding his boots, locking up the stable, and other contrivances of the like nature, he could not remember, from the moment he came into the house to the moment he left it, any one thing, wherein his inclination was not directly contradicted; as if the whole family had entered into a combination to torment him.

But, besides all this, it would be endless to recount the many foolish and ridiculous accidents I have observed among these unfortunate proselytes to ceremony. I have seen a duchess fairly knocked down, by the precipitancy of an officious coxcomb running to save her the trouble of opening a door. I remember, upon a birthday at court, a great lady was utterly desperate by a dish of sauce let fall by a page directly upon her head-dress and brocade, while she gave a sudden turn to her elbow upon some point of ceremony with the person who sat next her. Monsieur Buys, the Dutch envoy, whose politics and manners were much of a size, brought a son with him, about thirteen years old, to a great table at court. The boy and his father, whatever they put on their plates, they first offered round in order, to every person in the company; so that we could not get a minute's quiet during the whole dinner. At last their two plates happened to encounter, and with so much violence, that, being china, they broke in twenty pieces, and stained half the company with wet sweetmeats and cream.

There is a pedantry in manners, as in all arts and sciences; and sometimes in trades. Pedantry is properly the overrating any kind of knowledge we pretend to. And if that kind of knowledge be a trifle in itself, the pedantry is the greater. For which reason I look upon fiddlers, dancing-masters, heralds, masters of the ceremony, etc. to be greater pedants than Lipsius, or the elder Scaliger. With these kind of pedants, the court, while I knew it, was always plentifully stocked; I mean from the gentleman usher (at least) inclusive, downward to the gentleman porter; who are, generally speaking, the most insignificant race of people that this island can afford, and with the smallest tincture of good manners, which is the only trade they profess. For being wholly illiterate, and conversing chiefly with each other, they reduce the whole system of breeding within the forms and circles of their several offices; and as they are below the notice of ministers, they live and die in court under all revolutions with great obsequiousness to those who are in any degree of favour or credit, and with rudeness or insolence to everybody else. Whence I have long concluded, that good manners are not a plant of the court growth; for if they were, those people who have understandings directly of a level for such acquirements, and who have served such long apprenticeships to nothing else, would certainly have picked them up. For as to the great officers, who attend the prince's person or councils, or preside in his family, they are a transient body, who have no better a title to good manners than their neighbours, nor will probably have recourse to gentlemen ushers for instruction. So that I know little to be learnt at court upon this head, except in the material circumstance of dress; wherein the authority of the maids of honour must indeed be allowed to be almost equal to that of a favourite actress.

I remember a passage my Lord Bolingbroke told me, that going to receive Prince Eugene of Savoy at his landing, in order to conduct him immediately to the Queen, the prince said, he was much concerned that he could not see her Majesty that night; for Monsieur Hoffman (who was then by) had assured his Highness that he could not be admitted into her presence with a tied-up periwig; that his equipage was not arrived; and that he had endeavoured in vain to borrow a long one among all his valets and pages. My lord turned the matter into a jest, and brought the Prince to her Majesty; for which he was highly censured by the whole tribe of gentlemen ushers; among whom Monsieur Hoffman, an old dull resident of the Emperor's, had picked up this material point of ceremony; and which, I believe, was the best lesson he had learned in five-and-twenty years' residence.

I make a difference between good manners and good breeding; although, in order to vary my expression, I am sometimes forced to confound them. By the first, I only understand the art of remembering and applying certain settled forms of general behaviour. But good breeding is of a much larger extent; for besides an uncommon degree of literature sufficient to qualify a gentleman for reading a play, or a political pamphlet, it takes in a great compass of knowledge; no less than that of dancing, fighting, gaming, making the circle of Italy, riding the great horse, and speaking French; not to mention some other secondary, or subaltern accomplishments, which are more easily acquired. So that the difference between good breeding and good manners lies in this, that the former cannot be attained to by the best understandings, without study and labour; whereas a tolerable degree of reason will instruct us in every part of good manners, without other assistance.

I can think of nothing more useful upon this subject, than to point out some particulars, wherein the very essentials of good manners are concerned, the neglect or perverting of which doth very much disturb the good commerce of the world, by introducing a traffic of mutual uneasiness in most companies.

First, a necessary part of good manners, is a punctual observance of time at our own dwellings, or those of others, or at third places; whether upon matter of civility, business, or diversion; which rule, though it be a plain dictate of common reason, yet the greatest minister I ever knew was the greatest trespasser against it; by which all his business doubled upon him, and placed him in a continual arrear. Upon which I often used to rally him, as deficient in point of good manners. I have known more than one ambassador, and secretary of state with a very moderate portion of intellectuals, execute their offices with good success and applause, by the mere force of exactness and regularity. If you duly observe time for the service of another, it doubles the obligation; if upon your own account, it would be manifest folly, as well as ingratitude, to neglect it. If both are concerned, to make your equal or inferior attend on you, to his own disadvantage, is pride and injustice.

Ignorance of forms cannot properly be styled ill manners; because forms are subject to frequent changes; and consequently, being not founded upon reason, are beneath a wise man's regard. Besides, they vary in every country; and after a short period of time, very frequently in the same; so that a man who travels, must needs be at first a stranger to them in every court through which he passes; and perhaps at his return, as much a stranger in his own; and after all, they are easier to be remembered or forgotten than faces or names.

Indeed, among the many impertinences that superficial young men bring with them from abroad, this bigotry of forms is one of the principal, and more prominent than the rest; who look upon them not only as if they were matters capable of admitting of choice, but even as points of importance; and are therefore zealous on all occasions to introduce and propagate the new forms and fashions they have brought back with them. So that, usually speaking, the worst bred person in the company is a young traveller just returned from abroad.

Thoughts in Westminster Abbey

By Joseph Addison

When I am in a serious humour, I very often walk by myself in Westminster Abbey, where the gloominess of the place, and the use to which it is applied, with solemnity of the building, and the condition of the people who lie in it, are apt to fill the mind with a kind of melancholy, or rather thoughtfulness, that is not disagreeable, I yesterday passed a whole afternoon in the churchyard, the cloisters, and the church, amusing myself with the tombstones and inscriptions that I met with in those several regions of the dead. Most of them recorded nothing else of the buried person, but that he was born upon one day, and died upon another: that are common to all mankind. I could not but look upon these registers of existence, whether of brass or marble, as a kind of satire upon the departed persons, whether of brass or marble, as a kind of satire upon the departed persons; who had left no other memorial of them, but that they were born and that they died. They put me in mind of several persons mentioned in the battles of heroic poems, who have sounding names given them, for no other reason but that they may be killed, and are celebrated for nothing but being knocked on the head. The life of these men is finely described in Holy Writ by "the path of an arrow", which is immediately closed up and lost.

Upon my going into the church, I entertained myself with the digging of a grave; and saw in every shovelful of it that was thrown up, the fragment of a bone or skull intermix with a kind of fresh mouldering earth, that some time or other had a place in the composition of a human body. Upon this, I began to consider with myself what innumerable multitudes of people lay confused together under the pavement of that ancient cathedral; how men and women, friends and enemies, priests and soldiers, monks and prebendaries, were crumbled amongst one another, and blended together in the same common mass; how beauty, strength, and youth, with old age, weakness and deformity, lay undistinguished in the same promiscuous heap of matter.

After having thus surveyed this great magazine of mortality, as it were, in the lump; I examined it more particularly by the accounts which I found on several of the monuments which are raised in every quarter of that ancient fabric. Some of them were covered with such extravagant epitaphs, that, if it were possible for the dead person to be acquainted with them, he would blush at the praises which his friends have bestowed upon him. There are others so excessively modest, that they deliver the character of the person departed in Greek or Hebrew, and by that means are not understood once in a twelve month. In the poetical quarter, I found there were poets who had no monuments, and monuments which had no poets. I observed indeed that the present war had filled the church with many of these uninhabited monuments, which had been erected to the memory of persons whose bodies were perhaps buried in the plains of Blenheim, or in the bosom of the ocean.

  I could not but be very much delighted with several modern epitaphs, which are written with great elegance of expression and justness of thought, and therefore do honour to the living as well as to the dead. As a foreigner is very apt to conceive an idea of the ignorance or politeness of a nation, from the turn of their public monuments and inscriptions, they should be submitted to the perusal of men of learning and genius, before they are put in execution. Sir Cloudesly Shovell's monument has very often given me great offence: instead of the brave rough English Admiral, which was the distinguishing character of that plain gallant man, he is represented on his tomb by the figure of a beau, dressed in a long periwig, and reposing himself upon velvet cushions under a canopy of state. The inscription is answerable to the monument; for instead of celebrating the many remarkable actions he had performed in the service of his country, it acquaints us only with the manner of his death, in which it was impossible for him to reap any honour. The Dutch, whom we are apt to despise for want of genius, show an infinitely greater taste of antiquity and politeness in their buildings and works of this nature, than what we meet with in those of our own country. The monuments of their admirals, which have been erected at the public expense, represent them like themselves; and are adorned with rostral crowns and naval ornaments, with beautiful festoons of seaweed, shells, and coral.

  But to return to our subject. I have left the repository of our English kings for the contemplation of another day, when I shall find my mind disposed for so serious an amusement. I know that entertainments of this nature are apt to raise dark and dismal thoughts in timorous minds, and gloomy imaginations; but for my own part, though I am always serious, I do not know what it is to be melancholy; and can therefore take a view of nature in her deep and solemn scenes, with the same pleasure as in her most gay and delightful ones. By this means I can improve myself with those objects, which others consider with terror. When I look upon the tombs of the great, every emotion of envy dies in me; when I read the epitaphs of the beautiful, every inordinate desire goes out; when I meet with the grief of parents upon a tombstone, my heart melts with compassion; when I see the tomb of the parents themselves, I consider the vanity of grieving for those whom we must quickly follow; when I see kings lying by those who deposed them, when I consider rival wits placed side by side, or the holy men that divided the world with their contests and disputes, I reflect with sorrow and astonishment on the little competitions, factions and debates of mankind. When I read the several dates of the tombs, of some that died yesterday, and some six hundred years ago, I consider that great day when we shall all of us be contemporaries, and make our appearance together.

The Decay of Friendship

By Samuel Johnson

Life has no pleasure higher or nobler than that of friendship. It is painful to consider that this sublime enjoyment may be impaired or destroyed by innumerable causes, and that there is no human possession of which the duration is less certain.

Many have talked in very exalted language, of the perpetuity of friendship, of invincible constancy, and unalienable kindness; and some examples have been seen of men who have continued faithful to their earliest choice, and whose affection has predominated over changes of fortune, and contrariety of opinion.

But these instances are memorable, because they are rare. The friendship which is to be practiced or expected by common mortals, must take its rise from mutual pleasure, and must end when the power ceases of delighting each other.

Many accidents therefore may happen by which the ardor of kindness will be abated, without criminal baseness or contemptible inconstancy on either part. To give pleasure is not always in our power; and little does he know himself who believes that he can be always able to receive it.

Those who would gladly pass their days together may be separated by the different course of their affairs; and friendship, like love, is destroyed by long absence, though it may be increased by short intermissions. What we have missed long enough to want it, we value more when it is regained; but that which has been lost till it is forgotten, will be found at last with little gladness, and with still less if a substitute has supplied the place. A man deprived of the companion to whom he used to open his bosom, and with whom he shared the hours of leisure and merriment, feels the day at first hanging heavy on him; his difficulties oppress, and his doubts distract him; he sees time come and go without his wonted gratification, and all is sadness within, and solitude about him. But this uneasiness never lasts long; necessity produces expedients, new amusements are discovered, and new conversation is admitted.

No expectation is more frequently disappointed, than that which naturally arises in the mind from the prospect of meeting an old friend after long separation. We expect the attraction to be revived, and the coalition to be renewed; no man considers how much alteration time has made in himself, and very few inquire what effect it has had upon others. The first hour convinces them that the pleasure which they have formerly enjoyed, is forever at an end; different scenes have made different impressions; the opinions of both are changed; and that similitude of manners and sentiment is lost which confirmed them both in the approbation of themselves.

Friendship is often destroyed by opposition of interest, not only by the ponderous and visible interest which the desire of wealth and greatness forms and maintains, but by a thousand secret and slight competitions, scarcely known to the mind upon which they operate. There is scarcely any man without some favorite trifle which he values above greater attainments, some desire of petty praise which he cannot patiently suffer to be frustrated. This minute ambition is sometimes crossed before it is known, and sometimes defeated by wanton petulance; but such attacks are seldom made without the loss of friendship; for whoever has once found the vulnerable part will always be feared, and the resentment will burn on in secret, of which shame hinders the discovery.

This, however, is a slow malignity, which a wise man will obviate as inconsistent with quiet, and a good man will repress as contrary to virtue; but human happiness is sometimes violated by some more sudden strokes.

A dispute begun in jest upon a subject which a moment before was on both parts regarded with careless indifference, is continued by the desire of conquest, till vanity kindles into rage, and opposition rankles into enmity. Against this hasty mischief, I know not what security can be obtained; men will be sometimes surprised into quarrels; and though they might both haste into reconciliation, as soon as their tumult had subsided, yet two minds will seldom be found together, which can at once subdue their discontent, or immediately enjoy the sweets of peace without remembering the wounds of the conflict.

Friendship has other enemies. Suspicion is always hardening the cautious, and disgust repelling the delicate. Very slender differences will sometimes part those whom long reciprocation of civility or beneficence has united. Lonelove and Ranger retired into the country to enjoy the company of each other, and returned in six weeks, cold and petulant; Ranger's pleasure was to walk in the fields, and Lonelove's to sit in a bower; each had complied with the other in his turn, and each was angry that compliance had been exacted.

The most fatal disease of friendship is gradual decay, or dislike hourly increased by causes too slender for complaint, and too numerous for removal. Those who are angry may be reconciled; those who have been injured may receive a recompense: but when the desire of pleasing and willingness to be pleased is silently diminished, the renovation of friendship is hopeless; as, when the vital powers sink into languor, there is no longer any use of the physician.

Dream Children: A Reverie

By Charles Lamb

Children love to listen to stories about their elders, when they were children; to stretch their imagination to the conception of a traditionary great-uncle, or grandame, whom they never saw. It was in this spirit that my little ones crept about me the other evening to hear about their great-grandmother Field, who lived in a great house in Norfolk (a hundred times bigger than that in which they and papa lived) which had been the scene—so at least it was generally believed in that part of the country—of the tragic incidents which they had lately become familiar with from the ballad of *The Children in the Wood*. Certain it is that the whole story of the children and their cruel uncle was to be seen fairly carved out in wood upon the chimney-piece of the great hall, the whole story down to the Robin Redbreasts, till a foolish rich person pulled it down to set up a marble one of modern invention in its stead, with no story upon it.

Here Alice put out one of her dear mother's looks, too tender to be called upbraiding. Then I went on to say, how religious and how good their great-grandmother Field was, how beloved and respected by every body, though she was not indeed the mistress of this great house, but had only the charge of it (and yet in some respects she might be said to be the mistress of it too) committed to her by the owner, who preferred living in a newer and more fashionable mansion which he had purchased somewhere in the adjoining county; but still she lived in it in a manner as if it had been her own, and kept up the dignity of the great house in a sort while she lived, which afterwards came to decay, and was nearly pulled down, and all its old ornaments stripped and carried away to the owner's other house, where they were set up, and looked as awkward as if some one were to carry away the old tombs they had seen lately at the Abbey, and stick them up in Lady C.'s tawdry gilt drawing-room. Here John smiled, as much as to say, "that would be foolish indeed." And then I told how, when she came to die, her funeral was attended by a concourse of all the poor, and some of the gentry too, of the neighbourhood for many miles round, to show their respect for her memory, because she had been such a good and religious woman; so good indeed that she knew all the Psaltery by heart, ay, and a great part of the Testament besides. Here little Alice spread her hands. Then I told what a tall, upright, graceful person their great-grandmother Field once was; and how in her youth she was esteemed the best dancer—here Alice's little right foot played an involuntary movement, till, upon my looking grave, it desisted—the best dancer, I was saying, in the county, till a cruel disease, called a cancer, came, and bowed her down with pain; but it could never bend her good spirits, or make them stoop, but they were still upright, because she was so good and religious. Then I told how she was used to sleep by herself in a lone chamber of the great lone house; and how she believed that an apparition of two infants was to be seen at midnight gliding up and down the great staircase near where she slept, but she said, "those innocents would do her no harm;" and how frightened I used to be, though in those days I had my maid to sleep with me, because I was never half so good or religious as she—and yet I never saw the infants.

Here John expanded all his eye-brows and tried to look courageous. Then I told how good she was to all her grand-children, having us to the great-house in the holydays, where I in particular used to spend many hours by myself, in gazing upon the old busts of the Twelve Caesars, that had been Emperors of Rome, till the old marble heads would seem to live again, or I to be turned into marble with them; how I never could be tired with roaming about that huge mansion, with its vast empty rooms, with their worn-out hangings, fluttering tapestry, and carved oaken pannels, with the gilding almost rubbed out—sometimes in the spacious old-fashioned gardens, which I had almost to myself, unless when now and then a solitary gardening man would cross me—and how the nectarines and peaches hung upon the walls, without my ever offering to pluck them, because they were forbidden fruit, unless now and then,—and because I had more pleasure in strolling about among the old melancholy-looking yew trees, or the firs, and picking up the red berries, and the fir apples, which were good for nothing but to look at—or in lying about upon the fresh grass, with all the fine garden smells around me—or basking in the orangery, till I could almost fancy myself ripening too along with the oranges and the limes in that grateful warmth—or in watching the dace that darted to and fro in the fish-pond, at the bottom of the garden, with here and there a great sulky pike hanging midway down the water in silent state, as if it mocked at their impertinent friskings,—I had more pleasure in these busy-idle diversions than in all the sweet flavours of peaches, nectarines, oranges, and such like common baits of children.

Here John slyly deposited back upon the plate a bunch of grapes, which, not unobserved by Alice, he had meditated dividing with her, and both seemed willing to relinquish them for the present as irrelevant. Then in somewhat a more heightened tone, I told how, though their great-grandmother Field loved all her grand-children, yet in an especial manner she might be said to love their uncle, John L, because he was so handsome and spirited a youth, and a king to the rest of us; and, instead of moping about in solitary corners, like some of us, he would mount the most mettlesome horse he could get, when but an imp no bigger than themselves, and make it carry him half over the county in a morning, and join the hunters when there were any out—and yet he loved the old great house and gardens too, but had too much spirit to be always pent up within their boundaries—and how their uncle grew up to man's estate as brave as he was handsome, to the admiration of every body, but of their great-grandmother Field most especially; and how he used to carry me upon his back when I was a lame-footed boy—for he was a good bit older than me—many a mile when I could not walk for pain;—and how in after life he became lame-footed too, and I did not always (I fear) make allowances enough for him when he was impatient, and in pain, nor remember sufficiently how considerate he had been to me when I was lame-footed; and how when he died, though he had not been dead an hour, it seemed as if he had died a great while ago, such a distance there is betwixt life and death; and how I bore his death as I thought pretty well at first, but afterwards it haunted and haunted me; and though I did not cry or take it to heart as some do, and as I think he would have done if I had died, yet I missed him all day long, and knew not till then how much I had loved him. I missed his kindness, and I missed his crossness, and wished him to be alive again, to be quarrelling with him (for we quarreled sometimes), rather than not have him again, and was as uneasy without him, as he their poor uncle must have been when the doctor took off his limb.

Here the children fell a crying, and asked if their little mourning which they had on was not for uncle John, and they looked up, and prayed me not to go on about their uncle, but to tell them some stories about their pretty dead mother. Then I told how for seven long years, in hope sometimes, sometimes in despair, yet persisting ever, I courted the fair Alice; and, as much as children could understand, I explained to them what coyness, and difficulty, and denial meant in maidens—when suddenly, turning to Alice, the soul of the first Alice looked out at her eyes with such a reality of re-presentment, that I became in doubt which of them stood there before me, or whose that bright hair was; and while I stood gazing, both the children gradually grew fainter to my view, receding, and still receding till nothing at last but two mournful features were seen in the uttermost distance, which, without speech, strangely impressed upon me the effects of speech; "We are not of Alice, nor of thee, nor are we children at all. The children of Alice called Bartrum father. We are nothing; less than nothing, and dreams. We are only what might have been, and must wait upon the tedious shores of Lethe millions of ages before we have existence, and a name"—and immediately awaking, I found myself quietly seated in my bachelor arm-chair, where I had fallen asleep, with the faithful Bridget unchanged by my side—but John L. (or James Elia) was gone for ever.

On the Past and Future(An Excerpt)

By William Hazlitt

I myself am neither a king nor a shepherd: books have been my fleecy charge, and my thoughts have been my subjects. But these have found me sufficient employment at the time, and enough to think of for the time to come.

The passions contract and warp the natural progress of life. They paralyse all of it that is not devoted to their tyranny and caprice. This makes the difference between the laughing innocence of childhood, the pleasantness of youth, and the crabbedness of age. A load of cares lies like a weight of guilt upon the mind: so that a man of business often has all the air, the distraction and restlessness and hurry of feeling of a criminal. A knowledge of the world takes away the freedom and simplicity of thought as effectually as the contagion of its example. The artlessness and candour of our early years are open to all impressions alike, because the mind is not clogged and preoccupied with other objects. Our pleasures and our pains come single, make room for one another, and the spring of the mind is fresh and unbroken, its aspect clear and unsullied. Hence the tear forgot as soon as shed, the sunshine of the breast. But as we advance farther, the will gets greater head. We form violent antipathies and indulge exclusive preferences. We make up our minds to some one thing, and if we cannot have that, will have nothing. We are wedded to opinion, to fancy, to prejudice; which destroys the soundness of our judgments, and the serenity and buoyancy of our feelings. The chain of habit coils itself round the heart, like a serpent, to gnaw and stifle it. It grows rigid and callous; and for the softness and elasticity of childhood, full of proud flesh and obstinate tumours. The violence and perversity of our passions come in more and more to overlay our natural sensibility and well-grounded affections; and we screw ourselves up to aim only at those things which are neither desirable nor practicable. Thus life passes away in the feverish irritation of pursuit and the certainty of disappointment. By degrees, nothing but this morbid state of feeling satisfies us: and all common pleasures and cheap amusements are sacrificed to the demon of ambition, avarice, or dissipation. The machine is overwrought: the parching heat of the veins dries up and withers the flowers of Love, Hope, and Joy; and any pause, any release from the rack of ecstasy on which we are stretched, seems more insupportable than the pangs which we endure. We are suspended between tormenting desires and the horrors of ennui. The impulse of the will, like the wheels of a carriage going down hill, becomes too strong for the driver, Reason, and cannot be stopped nor kept within bounds. Some idea, some fancy, takes possession of the brain; and however ridiculous, however distressing, however ruinous, haunts us by a sort of fascination through life.

Not only is this principle of excessive irritability to be seen at work in our more turbulent passions and pursuits, but even in the formal study of arts and sciences, the same thing takes place, and undermines the repose and happiness of life. The eagerness of pursuit overcomes the satisfaction to result from the accomplishment. The mind is overstrained to attain its purpose; and when it is attained, the ease and alacrity necessary to enjoy it are gone. The irritation of action does not cease and go down with the occasion for it; but we are first uneasy to get to the end of our work, and then uneasy for want of something to do. The ferment of the brain does not of itself subside into pleasure and soft repose. Hence the disposition to strong stimuli observable in persons of much intellectual exertion to allay and carry off the over-excitement. The improvisatori poets (it is recorded by Spence in his *Anecdotes of Pope*) cannot sleep after an evening's continued display of their singular and difficult art. The rhymes keep running in their head in spite of themselves, and will not let them rest. Mechanics and labouring people never know what to do with themselves on a Sunday, though they return to their work with greater spirit for the relief, and look forward to it with pleasure all the week. Sir Joshua Reynolds was never comfortable out of his painting-room, and died of chagrin and regret because he could not paint on to the last moment of his life. He used to say that he could go on retouching a picture for ever, as long as it stood on his easel; but as soon as it was once fairly out of the house, he never wished to see it again. An ingenious artist of our own time has been heard to declare, that if ever the Devil got him into his clutches, he would set him to copy his own pictures. Thus secure, self-complacent retrospect to what is done is nothing, while the anxious, uneasy looking forward to what is to come is everything. We are afraid to dwell upon the past, lest it should retard our future progress; the indulgence of ease is fatal to excellence; and to succeed in life, we lose the ends of being!

On the Knocking at the Gate in *Macbeth*

By Thomas De Quincey

From my boyish days I had always felt a great perplexity on one point in *Macbeth*. It was this—the knocking at the gate, which succeeds to the murder of Duncan, produced to my feelings an effect for which I never could account. The effect was, that it reflected back upon the murderer a peculiar awfulness and a depth of solemnity; yet, however obstinately I endeavoured with my understanding to comprehend this, for many years I never could see why it should produce such an effect.

Here I pause for one moment, to exhort the reader never to pay any attention to his understanding, when it stands in opposition to any other faculty of his mind. The mere understanding, however useful and indispensable, is the meanest faculty in the human mind, and the most to be distrusted; and yet the great majority of people trust to nothing else, which may do for ordinary life, but not for philosophical purposes. Of this out of ten thousand instances that I might produce, I will cite one. Ask of any person whatsoever, who is not previously prepared for the demand by a knowledge of the perspective, to draw in the rudest way the commonest appearance which depends upon the laws of that science; as, for instance, to represent the effect of two walls standing at right angles to each other, or the appearance of the houses on each side of a street, as seen by a person looking down the street from one extremity.

Now in all cases, unless the person has happened to observe in pictures how it is that artists produce these effects, he will be utterly unable to make the smallest approximation to it. Yet why? For he has actually seen the effect every day of his life. The reason is that he allows his understanding to overrule his eyes. His understanding, which includes no intuitive knowledge of the laws of vision, can furnish him with no reason why a line which is known and can be proved to be a horizontal line, should not appear a horizontal line; a line that made any angle with the perpendicular, less than a right angle, would seem to him to indicate that his houses were all tumbling down together.

Accordingly, he makes the line of his houses a horizontal line, and fails, of course, to produce the effect demanded. Here, then, is one instance out of many, in which not only the understanding is allowed to overrule the eyes, but where the understanding is positively allowed to obliterate the eyes, as it were; for not only does the man believe the evidence of his understanding in opposition to that of his eyes, but (what is monstrous!) the idiot is not aware that his eyes ever gave such evidence. He does not know that he has seen (and therefore quoad his consciousness has not seen) that which he has seen every day of his life.

But to return from this digression, my understanding could furnish no reason why the knocking at the gate in *Macbeth* should produce any effect, direct or reflected. In fact, my understanding said positively that it could not produce any effect. But I knew better; I felt that it did; and I waited and clung to the problem until further knowledge should enable me to solve it. At length, in 1812, Mr. Williams made his debut on the stage of Ratcliffe Highway, and executed those unparalleled murders which have procured for him such a brilliant and undying reputation. On which murders, by the way, I must observe, that in one respect they have had an ill effect, by making the connoisseur in murder very fastidious in his taste, and dissatisfied by anything that has been since done in that line. All other murders look pale by the deep crimson of his; and, as an amateur once said to me in a querulous tone, "There has been absolutely nothing doing since his time, or nothing that's worth speaking of". But this is wrong; for it is unreasonable to expect all men to be great artists, and born with the genius of Mr. Williams. Now it will be remembered, that in the first of these murders (that of the Marrs), the same incident (of a knocking at the door) soon after the work of extermination was complete, did actually occur, which the genius of Shakespeare has invented; and all good judges, and the most eminent dilettanti, acknowledged the felicity of Shakespeare's suggestion, as soon as it was actually realized.

Here, then, was a fresh proof that I was right in relying on my own feeling, in opposition to my understanding; and I again set myself to study the problem; at length I solved it to my own satisfaction, and my solution is this. Murder, in ordinary cases, where the sympathy is wholly directed to the case of the murdered person, is an incident of coarse and vulgar horror; and for this reason, that it flings the interest exclusively upon the natural but ignoble instinct by which we cleave to life; an instinct which, as being indispensable to the primal law of self-preservation, is the same in kind (though different in degree) amongst all living creatures: this instinct, therefore, because it annihilates all distinctions, and degrades the greatest of men to the level of "the poor beetle that we tread on", exhibits human nature in its most abject and humiliating attitude. Such an attitude would little suit the purposes of the poet. What then must he do? He must throw the interest on the murderer.

Our sympathy must be with him (of course I mean a sympathy of comprehension, a sympathy by which we enter into his feelings, and are made to understand them, —not a sympathy of pity or approbation[①]). In the murdered person, all strife of thought, all flux and reflux of passion and of purpose, are crushed by one overwhelming panic; the fear of instant death smites him "with its petrific mace". But in the murderer, such a murderer as a poet will

---

[①] It seems almost ludicrous to guard and explain my use of a word, in a situation where it would naturally explain itself. But it has become necessary to do so, in consequence of the unscholarlike use of the word sympathy, at present so general, by which, instead of taking it in its proper sense, as the act of reproducing in our minds the feelings of another, whether for hatred, indignation, love, pity, or approbation, it is made a mere synonyme of the word pity; and hence, instead of saying "sympathy with another", many writers adopt the monstrous barbarism of "sympathy for another".

condescend to, there must be raging some great storm of passion—jealousy, ambition, vengeance, hatred—which will create a hell within him; and into this hell we are to look.

In *Macbeth*, for the sake of gratifying his own enormous and teeming faculty of creation, Shakespeare has introduced two murderers; and, as usual in his hands, they are remarkably discriminated; but, though in *Macbeth* the strife of mind is greater than in his wife, the tiger spirit not so awake, and his feelings caught chiefly by contagion from her,—yet, as both were finally involved in the guilt of murder, the murderous mind of necessity is finally to be presumed in both. This was to be expressed; and on its own account, as well as to make it a more proportionable antagonist to the unoffending nature of their victim, "the gracious Duncan", and adequately to expound "the deep damnation of his taking off", this was to be expressed with peculiar energy. We were to be made to feel that the human nature, i.e. the divine nature of love and mercy, spread through the hearts of all creatures, and seldom utterly withdrawn from man—was gone, vanished, extinct, and that the fiendish nature had taken its place.

And, as this effect is marvellously accomplished in the dialogues and soliloquies themselves, so it is finally consummated by the expedient under consideration; and it is to this that I now solicit the reader's attention. If the reader has ever witnessed a wife, daughter, or sister in a fainting fit, he may chance to have observed that the most affecting moment in such a spectacle is that in which a sigh and a stirring announce the recommencement of suspended life. Or, if the reader has ever been present in a vast metropolis, on the day when some great national idol was carried in funeral pomp to his grave, and chancing to walk near the course through which it passed, has felt powerfully in the silence and desertion of the streets, and in the stagnation of ordinary business, the deep interest which at that moment was possessing the heart of man—if all at once he should hear the death-like stillness broken up by the sound of wheels rattling away from the scene, and making known that the transitory vision was dissolved, he will be aware that at no moment was his sense of the complete suspension and pause in ordinary human concerns so full and affecting, as at that moment when the suspension ceases, and the goings-on of human life are suddenly resumed.

All action in any direction is best expounded, measured, and made apprehensible, by reaction. Now apply this to the case in *Macbeth*. Here, as I have said, the retiring of the human heart, and the entrance of the fiendish heart was to be expressed and made sensible. Another world has stept in; and the murderers are taken out of the region of human things, human purposes, human desires. They are transfigured: Lady Macbeth is "unsexed;" Macbeth has forgot that he was born of woman; both are conformed to the image of devils; and the world of devils is suddenly revealed. But how shall this be conveyed and made palpable? In order that a new world may step in, this world must for a time disappear. The murderers, and the murder must be insulated—cut off by an immeasurable gulf from the ordinary tide and succession of human affairs—locked up and sequestered in some deep recess; we must be made sensible that the world of ordinary life is suddenly arrested—laid asleep—tranced—racked into a dread armistice; time must be annihilated; relation to things without abolished; and all must pass self-withdrawn into a deep syncope and suspension of earthly passion. Hence it is, that when the deed is done, when the work of darkness is perfect, then the world of darkness passes away like a pageantry in the clouds: the knocking at the gate is heard; and it makes known audibly that the reaction has commenced; the human has made its reflux upon the fiendish; the pulses of life are beginning to beat again; and the re-establishment of the goings-on of the world in which we live, first makes us profoundly sensible of the awful parenthesis that had suspended them.

O mighty poet! Thy works are not as those of other men, simply and merely great works of art; but are also like the phenomena of nature, like the sun and the sea, the stars and the flowers; like frost and snow, rain and dew, hail-storm and thunder, which are to be studied with entire submission of our own faculties, and in the perfect faith that in them there can be no too much or too little, nothing useless or inert—but that, the farther we press in our discoveries, the more we shall see proofs of design and self-supporting arrangement where the careless eye had seen nothing but accident.

What I Have Lived for

By Bertrand Russell

Three passions, simple but overwhelmingly strong, have governed my life: the longing for love, the search for knowledge, and unbearable pity for the suffering of mankind. These passions, like great winds, have blown me hither and thither, in a wayward course, over a deep ocean of anguish, reaching to the verge of despair.

I have sought love, first, because it brings ecstasy—ecstasy so great that I would have sacrificed all the rest of life for a few hours of this joy. I have sought it, next, because it relieves loneliness—that terrible loneliness in which one shivering consciousness looks over the rim of the world into cold unfathomable lifeless abyss. I have sought it, finally, because in the union of love I have seen, in a mystic miniature, the prefiguring vision of the heaven that saints and poets have imagined. This is what I sought, and though it might seem too good for human life, this is what—at last—I have found.

With equal passion I have sought knowledge. I have wished to understand the hearts of men, I have wished to know why the stars shine. And I have tried to apprehend the Pythagorean power by which number holds away above the flux. A little of this, but not much, I have achieved.

Love and knowledge, so far as they were possible, led upward toward the heavens. But always pity brought me back to earth. Echoes of cries of pain reverberated in my heart. Children in famine, victims tortured by oppressors, helpless old people a hated burden to their sons, and the whole world of loneliness, poverty, and pain make a mockery of what human life should be. I long to alleviate the evil, but I cannot, and I too suffer.

This has been my life. I have found it worth living, and I would gladly live it again if the chance were offered to me.

The Death of the Moth

By Virginia Woolf

Moths that fly by day are not properly to be called moths; they do not excite that pleasant sense of dark autumn nights and ivy-blossom which the commonest yellow-underwing asleep in the shadow of the curtain never fails to rouse in us. They are hybrid creatures, neither gay like butterflies nor sombre like their own species. Nevertheless the present specimen, with his narrow hay-coloured wings, fringed with a tassel of the same colour, seemed to be content with life. It was a pleasant morning, mid-September, mild, benignant, yet with a keener breath than that of the summer months. The plough was already scoring the field opposite the window, and where the share had been, the earth was pressed flat and gleamed with moisture. Such vigour came rolling in from the fields and the down beyond that it was difficult to keep the eyes strictly turned upon the book. The rooks too were keeping one of their annual festivities; soaring round the tree tops until it looked as if a vast net with thousands of black knots in it had been cast up into the air; which, after a few moments sank slowly down upon the trees until every twig seemed to have a knot at the end of it. Then, suddenly, the net would be thrown into the air again in a wider circle this time, with the utmost clamour and vociferation, as though to be thrown into the air and settle slowly down upon the tree tops were a tremendously exciting experience.

The same energy which inspired the rooks, the ploughmen, the horses, and even, it seemed, the lean bare-backed downs, sent the moth fluttering from side to side of his square of the window-pane. One could not help watching him. One was, indeed, conscious of a queer feeling of pity for him. The possibilities of pleasure seemed that morning so enormous and so various that to have only a moth's part in life, and a day moth's at that, appeared a hard fate, and his zest in enjoying his meagre opportunities to the full, pathetic. He flew vigorously to one corner of his compartment, and, after waiting there a second, flew across to the other. What remained for him but to fly to a third corner and then to a fourth? That was all he could do, in spite of the size of the downs, the width of the sky, the far-off smoke of houses, and the romantic voice, now and then, of a steamer out at sea. What he could do he did. Watching him, it seemed as if a fibre, very thin but pure, of the enormous energy of the world had been thrust into his frail and diminutive body. As often as he crossed the pane, I could fancy that a thread of vital light became visible. He was little or nothing but life.

Yet, because he was so small, and so simple a form of the energy that was rolling in at the open window and driving its way through so many narrow and intricate corridors in my own brain and in those of other human beings, there was something marvelous as well as pathetic about him. It was as if someone had taken a tiny bead of pure life and decking it as lightly as possible with down and feathers, had set it dancing and zig-zagging to show us the true nature of life. Thus displayed one could not get over the strangeness of it. One is apt to forget all about life, seeing it humped and bossed and garnished and cumbered so that it has to move with the greatest circumspection and dignity. Again, the thought of all that life might have been had he been born in any other shape caused one to view his simple activities with a kind of pity.

After a time, tired by his dancing apparently, he settled on the window ledge in the sun, and, the queer spectacle being at an end, I forgot about him. Then, looking up, my eye was caught by him. He was trying to resume his dancing, but seemed either so stiff or so awkward that he could only flutter to the bottom of the window-pane; and when he tried to fly across it he failed. Being intent on other matters I watched these futile attempts for a time without thinking, unconsciously waiting for him to resume his flight, as one waits for a machine, that has stopped momentarily, to start again without considering the reason of its failure. After perhaps a seventh attempt he slipped from the wooden ledge and fell, fluttering his wings, on to his back on the window sill. The helplessness of his attitude roused me. It flashed upon me that he was in difficulties; he could no longer raise himself; his legs struggled vainly. But, as I stretched out a pencil, meaning to help him to right himself, it came over me that the failure and awkwardness were the approach of death. I laid the pencil down again.

The legs agitated themselves once more. I looked as if for the enemy against which he struggled. I looked out of doors. What had happened there? Presumably it was midday, and work in the fields had stopped. Stillness and quiet had replaced the previous animation. The birds had taken themselves off to feed in the brooks. The horses stood still. Yet the power was there all the same, massed outside indifferent, impersonal, not attending to anything in particular. Somehow it was opposed to the little hay-coloured moth. It was useless to try to do anything. One could only watch the extraordinary efforts made by those tiny legs against an oncoming doom which could, had it chosen, have submerged an entire city, not merely a city, but masses of human beings; nothing, I knew, had any chance against death. Nevertheless after a pause of exhaustion the legs fluttered again. It was superb this last protest, and so frantic that he succeeded at last in righting himself. One's sympathies, of course, were all on the side of life. Also, when there was nobody to care or to know, this gigantic effort on the part of an insignificant little moth, against a power of such magnitude, to retain what no one else valued or desired to keep, moved one strangely. Again, somehow, one saw life, a pure bead. I lifted the pencil again, useless though I knew it to be. But even as I did so, the unmistakable tokens of death showed themselves. The body relaxed, and instantly grew stiff. The struggle was over. The insignificant little creature now knew death. As I looked at the dead moth, this minute wayside triumph of so great a force over so mean an antagonist filled me with wonder. Just as life had been strange a few minutes before, so death was now as strange. The moth having righted himself now lay most decently and uncomplainingly composed. O yes, he seemed to say, death is stronger than I am.

The Sporting Spirit

By George Orwell

Now that the brief visit of the Dynamo football team has come to an end, it is possible to say publicly what many thinking people were saying privately before the Dynamos ever arrived. That is, that sport is an unfailing cause of ill-will, and that if such a visit as this had any effect at all on Anglo-Soviet relations, it could only be to make them slightly worse than before.

Even the newspapers have been unable to conceal the fact that at least two of the four matches played led to much bad feeling. At the Arsenal match, I am told by someone who was there, a British and a Russian player came to blows and the crowd booed the referee. The Glasgow match, someone else informs me, was simply a free-for-all from the start. And then there was the controversy, typical of our nationalistic age, about the composition of the Arsenal team. Was it really an all-England team, as claimed by the Russians, or merely a league team, as claimed by the British? And did the Dynamos end their tour abruptly in order to avoid playing an all-England team? As usual, everyone answers these questions according to his political predilections. Not quite everyone, however. I noted with interest, as an instance of the vicious passions that football provokes, that the sporting correspondent of the russophile News Chronicle took the anti-Russian line and maintained that Arsenal was not an all-England team. No doubt the controversy will continue to echo for years in the footnotes of history books. Meanwhile the result of the Dynamos' tour, in so far as it has had any result, will have been to create fresh animosity on both sides.

And how could it be otherwise? I am always amazed when I hear people saying that sport creates goodwill between the nations, and that if only the common peoples of the world could meet one another at football or cricket, they would have no inclination to meet on the battlefield. Even if one didn't know from concrete examples (the 1936 Olympic Games, for instance) that international sporting contests lead to orgies of hatred, one could deduce it from general principles.

Nearly all the sports practised nowadays are competitive. You play to win, and the game has little meaning unless you do your utmost to win. On the village green, where you pick up sides and no feeling of local patriotism is involved, it is possible to play simply for the fun and exercise; but as soon as the question of prestige arises, as soon as you feel that you and some larger unit will be disgraced if you lose, the most savage combative instincts are aroused. Anyone who has played even in a school football match knows this. At the international level, sport is frankly mimic warfare. But the significant thing is not the behaviour of the players but the attitude of the spectators; and, behind the spectators, of the nations who work themselves into furies over these absurd contests, and seriously believe—at any rate for short periods—that running, jumping and kicking a ball are tests of national virtue.

Even a leisurely game like cricket, demanding grace rather than strength, can cause much ill-will, as we saw in the controversy over bodyline bowling and over the rough tactics of the Australian team that visited England in 1921. Football, a game in which everyone gets hurt and every nation has its own style of play which seems unfair to foreigners, is far worse. Worst of all is boxing. One of the most horrible sights in the world is a fight between white and coloured boxers before a mixed audience. But a boxing audience is always disgusting, and the behaviour of the women, in particular, is such that the army, I believe, does not allow them to attend its contests. At any rate, two or three years ago, when Home Guards and regular troops were holding a boxing tournament, I was placed on guard at the door of the hall, with orders to keep the women out.

In England, the obsession with sport is bad enough, but even fiercer passions are aroused in young countries where games playing and nationalism are both recent developments. In countries like India or Burma, it is necessary at football matches to have strong cordons of police to keep the crowd from invading the field. In Burma, I have seen the supporters of one side break through the police and disable the goalkeeper of the opposing side at a critical moment. The first big football match that was played in Spain about fifteen years ago led to an uncontrollable riot. As soon as strong feelings of rivalry are aroused, the notion of playing the game according to the rules always vanishes. People want to see one side on top and the other side humiliated, and they forget that victory gained through cheating or through the intervention of the crowd is meaningless. Even when the spectators don't intervene physically, they try to influence the game by cheering their own side and "rattling" opposing players with boos and insults. Serious sport has nothing to do with fair play. It is bound up with hatred, jealousy, boastfulness, disregard of all rules and sadistic pleasure in witnessing violence: in other words it is war minus the shooting.

Instead of blah-blahing about the clean, healthy rivalry of the football field and the great part played by the Olympic Games in bringing the nations together, it is more useful to inquire how and why this modern cult of sport arose. Most of the games we now play are of ancient origin, but sport does not seem to have been taken very seriously between Roman times and the nineteenth century. Even in the English public schools the games cult did not start till the later part of the last century. Dr. Arnold, generally regarded as the founder of the modern public school, looked on games as simply a waste of time. Then, chiefly in England and the United States, games were built up into a heavily-financed activity, capable of attracting vast crowds and rousing savage passions, and the infection spread from country to country. It is the most violently combative sports, football and boxing, that have spread the widest. There cannot be much doubt that the whole thing is bound up with the rise of nationalism—that is, with the lunatic modern habit of identifying oneself with large power units and seeing everything in terms of competitive prestige. Also, organised games are more likely to flourish in urban communities where the average human being lives a sedentary or at least a confined life, and does not get much opportunity for creative labour. In a rustic community a boy or young man works off a good deal of his surplus energy by walking, swimming, snowballing, climbing trees, riding horses, and by various sports involving cruelty to animals, such as fishing, cockfighting and ferreting for rats. In a big town one must indulge in group activities if one wants an outlet for one's physical strength or for one's sadistic impulses. Games are taken seriously in London and New York, and they were taken seriously in Rome and Byzantium: in the Middle Ages they were played, and probably played with much physical brutality, but they were not mixed up with politics nor a cause of group hatreds.

If you wanted to add to the vast fund of ill-will existing in the world at this moment, you could hardly do it better than by a series of football matches between Jews and Arabs, Germans and Czechs, Indians and British, Russians and Poles, and Italians and Jugoslavs, each match to be watched by a mixed audience of 100,000 spectators. I do not, of course, suggest that sport is one of the main causes of international rivalry; big-scale sport is itself, I think, merely another effect of the causes that have produced nationalism. Still, you do make things worse by sending forth a team of eleven men, labelled as national champions, to do battle against some rival team, and allowing it to be felt on all sides that whichever nation is defeated will "lose face".

I hope, therefore, that we shan't follow up the visit of the Dynamos by sending a British team to the USSR. If we must do so, then let us send a second-rate team which is sure to be beaten and cannot be claimed to represent Britain as a whole. There are quite enough real causes of trouble already, and we need not add to them by encouraging young men to kick each other on the shins amid the roars of infuriated spectators.

First Snow

By John Boynton Priestley

When I got up this morning, the world was a chilled hollow of dead white and faint blues. The light that came through the windows was very queer, and it contrived to make the familiar business of splashing and shaving and brushing and dressing very queer too. Then the sun came out, and by the time I had sat down to breakfast, it was shining bravely and flushing the snow with delicate pinks. The dining-room window had been transformed into a lovely Japanese print. The little plum-tree outside, with the faintly flushed snow lining its boughs and artfully disposed along its trunk, stood in full sunlight. An hour or two later, everything was a cold glitter of white and blue. The world had completely changed again. The little Japanese prints had all vanished. I looked out of my study window, over the garden, the meadow, to the low hills beyond, and the ground was one long glare, the sky was steely, and all the trees so many black and sinister shapes. There was indeed something curiously sinister about the whole prospect. It was as if our kindly countryside, closed to the very heart of England, had been turned into a cruel steppe. At any moment, it seemed, a body of horsemen might be seen breaking out from the black copse, so many instruments of tyranny, and shots might be heard and some distant patch of snow be reddened. It was that kind of landscape.

Now it has changed again. The glare has gone and no touch of the sinister remains. But the snow is falling heavily, in great soft flakes, so that you can hardly see across the shallow valley, and the roofs are thick and the trees all bending, and the weathercock of the village church, still to be seen through the grey loaded air, has become some creature out of Hans Andersen. From my study, which is apart from the house and faces it, I can see the children flattening their noses against the nursery window, and there is running through my head a jangle of rhyme I used to repeat when I was a child and flattened my nose against the cold window to watch the falling snow:

Snow, snow faster,
White alabaster!
Killing geese in Scotland,
Sending feathers here!

This morning, when I first caught sight of the unfamiliar whitened world, I could not help wishing that we had snow oftener, that English winters were more wintry. How delightful it would be, I thought, to have months of clean snow and a landscape sparkling with frost instead of innumerable grey featureless days of rain and raw winds. I began to envy my friends in such places as the Eastern States of America and Canada, who can count upon a solid winter every year and know that the snow will arrive by a certain date and will remain, without degenerating into black slush, until Spring is close at hand. To have snow and frost and yet a clear sunny sky and air as crisp as a biscui—this seemed to me happiness indeed. And then I saw that it would never do for us. We should be sick of it in a week. After the first day, the magic would be gone and there would be nothing left but the unchanging glare of the day and the bitter cruel nights. It is not the snow itself, the sight of the blanketed world, that is so enchanting, but the first coming of the snow, the sudden and silent change. Out of the relations, for ever shifting and unanticipated, of wind and water comes a magical event. Who would change this state of things for a steadily recurring round, an earth governed by the calendar? It has been well said that while other countries have a climate, we alone in England have weather. There is nothing duller than climate, which can be converted into a topic only by scientists and hypochondriacs. But weather is our earth's Cleopatra, and it is not to be wondered at that we, who must share her gigantic moods, should be for ever talking about her. Once we were settled in America, Siberia, Australia, where there is nothing but a steady pact between climate and the calendar, we should regret her very naughtinesses, her willful pranks, her gusts of rage, and sudden tears. Waking in a morning would no longer be an adventure. Our weather may be fickle, but it is no more fickle than we are, and only matches our inconstancy with her changes. Sun, wind, snow, rain, how welcome they are at first and how soon we grow weary of them! If this snow lasts a week, I shall be heartily sick of it and glad to speed its going. But its coming has been an event. Today has had a quality, an atmosphere, quite different from that of yesterday, and I have moved through it feeling a slightly different person, as if I were staying with new friends or had suddenly arrived in Norway. A man might easily spend five hundred pounds trying to break the crust of indifference in his mind, and yet feel less than I did this morning.

Advice to a Young Man on the Choice of a Mistress

By Benjamin Franklin

June 25, 1745

My dear Friend,

    I know of no medicine fit to diminish the violent natural inclinations you mention; and if I did, I think I should not communicate it to you. Marriage is the proper remedy. It is the most natural state of man, and therefore the state in which you are most likely to find solid happiness. Your reasons against entering into it at present, appear to me not well founded. The circumstantial advantages you have in view by postponing it, are not only uncertain, but they are small in comparison with that of the thing itself, the being married and settled. It is the man and woman united that make the complete human being. Separate, she wants his force of body and strength of reason; he, her fitness, sensibility, and acute discernment. Together they are more likely to succeed in the world. A single man has not nearly the value he would have in the state of union. He is an incomplete animal. He resembles the odd half of a pair of scissors. If you get a prudent healthy wife, your industry in your profession, with her good economy, will be a fortune sufficient.

    But if you will not take this counsel and persist in thinking a commerce with the sex inevitable, then I repeat my former advice, that in all your amours you should prefer old women to young ones. You call this a paradox, and demand my reasons. They are these:

    1. Because as they have more knowledge of the world and their minds are better stored with observations, their conversation is more improving and more lastingly agreeable.

    2. Because when women cease to be handsome they study to be good. To maintain their influence over men, they supply the diminution of beauty by an augmentation of utility. They learn to do a thousand services small and great, and are the most tender and useful of all friends when you are sick. Thus they continue amiable. And hence there is hardly such a thing to be found as an old woman who is not a good woman.

    3. Because there is no hazard of children, which irregularly produc'd may be attended with much inconvenience.

    4. Because through more experience, they are more prudent and discreet in conducting an intrigue to prevent suspicion. The commerce with them is therefore safer with regard to your reputation. And with regard to theirs, if the affair should happen to be known, considerate people might be rather inclin'd to excuse an old woman, who would kindly take care of a young man,

form his manners by her good counsels, and prevent his ruining his health and fortune among mercenary prostitutes.

5. Because in every animal that walks upright, the deficiency of the fluids that fill the muscles appears first in the highest part: the face first grows lank and wrinkled; then the neck; then the breast and arms; the lower parts continuing to the last as plump as ever; so that covering all above with a basket, and regarding only what is below the girdle, it is impossible of two women to know an old from a young one. And as in the dark all cats are gray, the pleasure of corporal enjoyment with an old woman is at least equal, and frequently superior, every knack being by practice capable of improvement.

6. Because the sin is less. The debauching a virgin may be her ruin, and make her for life unhappy.

7. Because the compunction is less. The having made a young girl miserable may give you frequent bitter reflection; none of which can attend the making an old woman happy.

8. [thly and lastly] They are so grateful!!

Thus much for my paradox. But still I advise you to marry directly; being sincerely.

Your affectionate friend,
B. Franklin

Nature

By Ralph Waldo Emerson

To go into solitude, a man needs to retire as much from his chamber as from society. I am not solitary whilst I read and write, though nobody is with me. But if a man would be alone, let him look at the stars. The rays that come from those heavenly worlds, will separate between him and what he touches. One might think the atmosphere was made transparent with this design, to give man, in the heavenly bodies, the perpetual presence of the sublime. Seen in the streets of cities, how great they are! If the stars should appear one night in a thousand years, how would men believe and adore; and preserve for many generations the remembrance of the city of God which had been shown! But every night come out these envoys of beauty, and light the universe with their admonishing smile.

The stars awaken a certain reverence, because though always present, they are inaccessible; but all natural objects make a kindred impression, when the mind is open to their influence. Nature never wears a mean appearance. Neither does the wisest man extort her secret, and lose his curiosity by finding out all her perfection. Nature never became a toy to a wise spirit. The flowers, the animals, the mountains, reflected the wisdom of his best hour, as much as they had delighted the simplicity of his childhood.

When we speak of nature in this manner, we have a distinct but most poetical sense in the mind. We mean the integrity of impression made by manifold natural objects. It is this which distinguishes the stick of timber of the wood-cutter, from the tree of the poet. The charming landscape which I saw this morning, is indubitably made up of some twenty or thirty farms. Miller owns this field, Locke that, and Manning the woodland beyond. But none of them owns the landscape. There is a property in the horizon which no man has but he whose eye can integrate all the parts, that is, the poet. This is the best part of these men's farms, yet to this their warranty-deeds give no title.

To speak truly, few adult persons can see nature. Most persons do not see the sun. At least they have a very superficial seeing. The sun illuminates only the eye of the man, but shines into the eye and the heart of the child. The lover of nature is he whose inward and outward senses are still truly adjusted to each other; who has retained the spirit of infancy even into the era of manhood. His intercourse with heaven and earth, becomes part of his daily food. In the presence of nature, a wild delight runs through the man, in spite of real sorrows. Nature says, he is my creature, and maugre all his impertinent griefs, he shall be glad with me. Not the sun or the summer alone, but every hour and season yields its tribute of delight; for every hour and change corresponds to and authorizes a different state of the mind, from breathless noon to grimmest midnight. Nature is a setting that fits equally well a comic or a mourning piece. In good health, the air is a cordial of incredible virtue. Crossing a bare common, in snow puddles, at twilight, under a clouded sky, without having in my thoughts any occurrence of special good fortune, I have enjoyed a perfect exhilaration. I am glad to the brink of fear. In the woods too, a man casts off his years, as the snake his slough, and at what period soever of life, is always a child. In the woods, is perpetual youth. Within these plantations of God, a decorum and sanctity reign, a perennial festival is dressed, and the guest sees not how he should tire of them in a thousand years. In the woods, we return to reason and faith. There I feel that nothing can befall me in life,—no disgrace, no calamity, (leaving me my eyes,) which nature cannot repair. Standing on the bare ground,—my head bathed by the blithe air, and uplifted into infinite space,—all mean egotism vanishes. I become a transparent eye-ball; I am nothing; I see all; the currents of the Universal Being circulate through me; I am part or particle of God. The name of the nearest friend sounds then foreign and accidental: to be brothers, to be acquaintances,—master or servant, is then a trifle and a disturbance. I am the lover of uncontained and immortal beauty. In the wilderness, I find something more dear and connate than in streets or villages. In the tranquil landscape, and especially in the distant line of the horizon, man beholds somewhat as beautiful as his own nature.

The greatest delight which the fields and woods minister, is the suggestion of an occult relation between man and the vegetable. I am not alone and unacknowledged. They nod to me, and I to them. The waving of the boughs in the storm, is new to me and old. It takes me by surprise, and yet is not unknown. Its effect is like that of a higher thought or a better emotion coming over me, when I deemed I was thinking justly or doing right.

Yet it is certain that the power to produce this delight, does not reside in nature, but in man, or in a harmony of both. It is necessary to use these pleasures with great temperance. For, nature is not always tricked in holiday attire, but the same scene which yesterday breathed perfume and glittered as for the frolic of the nymphs, is overspread with melancholy today. Nature always wears the colors of the spirit. To a man laboring under calamity, the heat of his own fire hath sadness in it. Then, there is a kind of contempt of the landscape felt by him who has just lost by death a dear friend. The sky is less grand as it shuts down over less worth in the population.

Where I Lived, and What I Lived for

By Henry David Thoreau

At a certain season of our life we are accustomed to consider every spot as the possible site of a house. I have thus surveyed the country on every side within a dozen miles of where I live. In imagination I have bought all the farms in succession, for all were to be bought, and I knew their price. I walked over each farmer's premises, tasted his wild apples, discoursed on husbandry with him, took his farm at his price, at any price, mortgaging it to him in my mind; even put a higher price on it—took everything but a deed of it—took his word for his deed, for I dearly love to talk—cultivated it, and him too to some extent, I trust, and withdrew when I had enjoyed it long enough, leaving him to carry it on. This experience entitled me to be regarded as a sort of real-estate broker by my friends. Wherever I sat, there I might live, and the landscape radiated from me accordingly. What is a house but a sedes, a seat?—Better if a country seat. I discovered many a site for a house not likely to be soon improved, which some might have thought too far from the village, but to my eyes the village was too far from it. Well, there I might live, I said; and there I did live, for an hour, a summer and a winter life; saw how I could let the years run off, buffet the winter through, and see the spring come in. The future inhabitants of this region, wherever they may place their houses, may be sure that they have been anticipated. An afternoon sufficed to lay out the land into orchard, wood-lot, and pasture, and to decide what fine oaks or pines should be left to stand before the door, and whence each blasted tree could be seen to the best advantage; and then I let it lie, fallow, perchance, for a man is rich in proportion to the number of things which he can afford to let alone.

My imagination carried me so far that I even had the refusal of several farms—the refusal was all I wanted—but I never got my fingers burned by actual possession. The nearest that I came to actual possession was when I bought the Hollowell place, and had begun to sort my seeds, and collected materials with which to make a wheelbarrow to carry it on or off with; but before the owner gave me a deed of it, his wife—every man has such a wife—changed her mind and wished to keep it, and he offered me ten dollars to release him. Now, to speak the truth, I had but ten cents in the world, and it surpassed my arithmetic to tell, if I was that man who had ten cents, or who had a farm, or ten dollars, or all together. However, I let him keep the ten dollars and the farm too, for I had carried it far enough; or rather, to be generous, I sold him the farm for just what I gave for it, and, as he was not a rich man, made him a present of ten dollars, and still had my ten cents, and seeds, and materials for a wheelbarrow left. I found thus that I had been a rich man without any damage to my poverty. But I retained the landscape, and I have since annually carried off what it yielded without a wheelbarrow. With respect to landscapes,

"I am monarch of all I survey,

My right there is none to dispute."

I have frequently seen a poet withdraw, having enjoyed the most valuable part of a farm, while the crusty farmer supposed that he had got a few wild apples only. Why, the owner does not know it for many years when a poet has put his farm in rhyme, the most admirable kind of invisible fence, has fairly impounded it, milked it, skimmed it, and got all the cream, and left the farmer only the skimmed milk.

The real attractions of the Hollowell farm, to me, were: its complete retirement, being, about two miles from the village, half a mile from the nearest neighbor, and separated from the highway by a broad field; its bounding on the river, which the owner said protected it by its fogs from frosts in the spring, though that was nothing to me; the gray color and ruinous state of the house and barn, and the dilapidated fences, which put such an interval between me and the last occupant; the hollow and lichen-covered apple trees, nawed by rabbits, showing what kind of neighbors I should have; but above all, the recollection I had of it from my earliest voyages up the river, when the house was concealed behind a dense grove of red maples, through which I heard the house-dog bark. I was in haste to buy it, before the proprietor finished getting out some rocks, cutting down the hollow apple trees, and grubbing up some young birches which had sprung up in the pasture, or, in short, had made any more of his improvements. To enjoy these advantages I was ready to carry it on; like Atlas, to take the world on my shoulders—I never heard what compensation he received for that—and do all those things which had no other motive or excuse but that I might pay for it and be unmolested in my possession of it; for I knew all the while that it would yield the most abundant crop of the kind I wanted, if I could only afford to let it alone. But it turned out as I have said.

All that I could say, then, with respect to farming on a large scale—I have always cultivated a garden—was, that I had had my seeds ready. Many think that seeds improve with age. I have no doubt that time discriminates between the good and the bad; and when at last I shall plant, I shall be less likely to be disappointed. But I would say to my fellows, once for all, As long as possible live free and uncommitted. It makes but little difference whether you are committed to a farm or the county jail.

Old Cato, whose "De Re Rustica" is my "Cultivator", says—and the only translation I have seen makes sheer nonsense of the passage— "When you think of getting a farm turn it thus in your mind, not to buy greedily; nor spare your pains to look at it, and do not think it enough to go round it once. The oftener you go there the more it will please you, if it is good". I think I shall not buy greedily, but go round and round it as long as I live, and be buried in it first, that it may please me the more at last.

The present was my next experiment of this kind, which I purpose to describe more at length, for convenience putting the experience of two years into one. As I have said, I do not propose to write an ode to dejection, but to brag as lustily as chanticleer in the morning, standing on his roost, if only to wake my neighbors up.

When first I took up my abode in the woods, that is, began to spend my nights as well as days there, which, by accident, was on Independence Day, or the Fourth of July, 1845, my house was not finished for winter, but was merely a defence against the rain, without plastering or chimney, the walls being of rough, weather-stained boards, with wide chinks, which made it cool at night. The upright white hewn studs and freshly planed door and window casings gave it a clean and airy look, especially in the morning, when its timbers were saturated with dew, so that I fancied that by noon some sweet gum would exude from them. To my imagination it retained throughout the day more or less of this auroral character, reminding me of a certain house on a mountain which I had visited a year before. This was an airy and unplastered cabin, fit to entertain a travelling god, and where a goddess might trail her garments. The winds which passed over my dwelling were such as sweep over the ridges of mountains, bearing the broken strains, or celestial parts only, of terrestrial music. The morning wind forever blows, the poem of creation is uninterrupted; but few are the ears that hear it. Olympus is but the outside of the earth everywhere.

The only house I had been the owner of before, if I except a boat, was a tent, which I used occasionally when making excursions in the summer, and this is still rolled up in my garret; but the boat, after passing from hand to hand, has gone down the stream of time. With this more substantial shelter about me, I had made some progress toward settling in the world. This frame, so slightly clad, was a sort of crystallization around me, and reacted on the builder. It was suggestive somewhat as a picture in outlines. I did not need to go outdoors to take the air, for the atmosphere within had lost none of its freshness. It was not so much within doors as behind a door where I sat, even in the rainiest weather. The Harivansa says, "An abode without birds is like a meat without seasoning". Such was not my abode, for I found myself suddenly neighbor to the birds; not by having imprisoned one, but having caged myself near them. I was not only nearer to some of those which commonly frequent the garden and the orchard, but to those smaller and more thrilling songsters of the forest which never, or rarely, serenade a villager—the wood thrush, the veery, the scarlet tanager, the field sparrow, the whip-poor-will, and many others.

I was seated by the shore of a small pond, about a mile and a half south of the village of Concord and somewhat higher than it, in the midst of an extensive wood between that town and Lincoln, and about two miles south of that our only field known to fame, Concord Battle Ground; but I was so low in the woods that the opposite shore, half a mile off, like the rest, covered with wood, was my most distant horizon. For the first week, whenever I looked out on the pond it impressed me like a tarn high up on the side of a mountain, its bottom far above the surface of other lakes, and, as the sun arose, I saw it throwing off its nightly clothing of mist, and here and there, by degrees, its soft ripples or its smooth reflecting surface was revealed, while the mists, like ghosts, were stealthily withdrawing in every direction into the woods, as at the breaking up of some nocturnal conventicle. The very dew seemed to hang upon the trees later into the day than usual, as on the sides of mountains.

This small lake was of most value as a neighbor in the intervals of a gentle rain-storm in August, when, both air and water being perfectly still, but the sky overcast, mid-afternoon had all the serenity of evening, and the wood thrush sang around, and was heard from shore to shore. A lake like this is never smoother than at such a time; and the clear portion of the air above it being, shallow and darkened by clouds, the water, full of light and reflections, becomes a lower heaven itself so much the more important. From a hill-top near by, where the wood had been recently cut off, there was a pleasing vista southward across the pond, through a wide indentation in the hills which form the shore there, where their opposite sides sloping toward each other suggested a stream flowing out in that direction through a wooded valley, but stream there was none. That way I looked between and over the near green hills to some distant and higher ones in the horizon, tinged with blue. Indeed, by standing on tiptoe I could catch a glimpse of some of the peaks of the still bluer and more distant mountain ranges in the northwest, those true-blue coins from heaven's own mint, and also of some portion of the village. But in other directions, even from this point, I could not see over or beyond the woods which surrounded me. It is well to have some water in your neighborhood, to give buoyancy to and float the earth. One value even of the smallest well is, that when you look into it you see that earth is not continent but insular. This is as important as that it keeps butter cool. When I looked across the pond from this peak toward the Sudbury meadows, which in time of flood I distinguished elevated perhaps by a mirage in their seething valley, like a coin in a basin, all the earth beyond the pond appeared like a thin crust insulated and floated even by this small sheet of interverting water, and I was reminded that this on which I dwelt was but dry land.

Though the view from my door was still more contracted, I did not feel crowded or confined in the least. There was pasture enough for my imagination. The low shrub oak plateau to which the opposite shore arose stretched away toward the prairies of the West and the steppes of Tartary, affording ample room for all the roving families of men. "There are none happy in the world but beings who enjoy freely a vast horizon"—said Damodara, when his herds required new and larger pastures.

Both place and time were changed, and I dwelt nearer to those parts of the universe and to those eras in history which had most attracted me. Where I lived was as far off as many a region viewed nightly by astronomers. We are wont to imagine rare and delectable places in some remote and more celestial corner of the system, behind the constellation of Cassiopeia's Chair, far from noise and disturbance. I discovered that my house actually had its site in such a withdrawn, but forever new and unprofaned, part of the universe. If it were worth the while to settle in those parts near to the Pleiades or the Hyades, to Aldebaran or Altair, then I was really there, or at an equal remoteness from the life which I had left behind, dwindled and twinkling with as fine a ray to my nearest neighbor, and to be seen only in moonless nights by him. Such was that part of creation where I had squatted;

"There was a shepherd that did live,

And held his thoughts as high

As were the mounts whereon his flocks

Did hourly feed him by."

What should we think of the shepherd's life if his flocks always wandered to higher pastures than his thoughts?

Every morning was a cheerful invitation to make my life of equal simplicity, and I may say innocence, with Nature herself. I have been as sincere a worshipper of Aurora as the Greeks. I got up early and bathed in the pond; that was a religious exercise, and one of the best things which I did. They say that characters were engraven on the bathing tub of King Tchingthang to this effect: "Renew thyself completely each day; do it again, and again, and forever again". I can understand that. Morning brings back the heroic ages. I was as much affected by the faint hum of a mosquito making its invisible and unimaginable tour through my apartment at earliest dawn, when I was sitting with door and windows open, as I could be by any trumpet that ever sang of fame. It was Homer's requiem; itself an Iliad and Odyssey in the air, singing its own wrath and wanderings. There was something cosmical about it; a standing advertisement, till forbidden, of the everlasting vigor and fertility of the world. The morning, which is the most memorable season of the day, is the awakening hour. Then there is least somnolence in us; and for an hour, at least, some part of us awakes which slumbers all the rest of the day and night. Little is to be expected of that day, if it can be called a day, to which we are not awakened by our Genius, but by the mechanical nudgings of some servitor, are not awakened by our own newly acquired force and aspirations from within, accompanied by the undulations of celestial music, instead of factory bells, and a fragrance filling the air—to a higher life than we fell asleep from; and thus the darkness bear its fruit, and prove itself to be good, no less than the light. That man who does not believe that each day contains an earlier, more sacred, and auroral hour than he has yet profaned, has despaired of life, and is pursuing a descending and darkening way. After a partial cessation of his sensuous life, the soul of man, or its organs rather, are reinvigorated each day, and his Genius tries again what noble life it can make. All memorable events, I should say, transpire in morning time and in a morning atmosphere. The Vedas say, "All intelligences awake with the morning". Poetry and art, and the fairest and most memorable of the actions of men, date from such an hour. All poets and heroes, like Memnon, are the children of Aurora, and emit their music at sunrise. To him whose elastic and vigorous thought keeps pace with the sun, the day is a perpetual morning. It matters not what the clocks say or the attitudes and labors of men. Morning is when I am awake and there is a dawn in me. Moral reform is the effort to throw off sleep. Why is it that men give so poor an account of their day if they have not been slumbering? They are not such poor calculators. If they had not been overcome with drowsiness, they would have performed something. The millions are awake enough for physical labor; but only one in a million is awake enough for effective intellectual exertion, only one in a hundred millions to a poetic or divine life. To be awake is to be alive. I have never yet met a man who was quite awake. How could I have looked him in the face?

We must learn to reawaken and keep ourselves awake, not by mechanical aids, but by an infinite expectation of the dawn, which does not forsake us in our soundest sleep. I know of no more encouraging fact than the unquestionable ability of man to elevate his life by a conscious endeavor. It is something to be able to paint a particular picture, or to carve a statue, and so to make a few objects beautiful; but it is far more glorious to carve and paint the very atmosphere and medium through which we look, which morally we can do. To affect the quality of the day, that is the highest of arts. Every man is tasked to make his life, even in its details, worthy of the contemplation of his most elevated and critical hour. If we refused, or rather used up, such paltry information as we get, the oracles would distinctly inform us how this might be done.

I went to the woods because I wished to live deliberately, to front only the essential facts of life, and see if I could not learn what it had to teach, and not, when I came to die, discover that I had not lived. I did not wish to live what was not life, living is so dear; nor did I wish to practise resignation, unless it was quite necessary. I wanted to live deep and suck out all the marrow of life, to live so sturdily and Spartan-like as to put to rout all that was not life, to cut a broad swath and shave close, to drive life into a corner, and reduce it to its lowest terms, and, if it proved to be mean, why then to get the whole and genuine meanness of it, and publish its meanness to the world; or if it were sublime, to know it by experience, and be able to give a true account of it in my next excursion. For most men, it appears to me, are in a strange uncertainty about it, whether it is of the devil or of God, and have somewhat hastily concluded that it is the chief end of man here to "glorify God and enjoy him forever".

Still we live meanly, like ants; though the fable tells us that we were long ago changed into men; like pygmies we fight with cranes; it is error upon error, and clout upon clout, and our best virtue has for its occasion a superfluous and evitable wretchedness. Our life is frittered away by detail. An honest man has hardly need to count more than his ten fingers, or in extreme cases he may add his ten toes, and lump the rest. Simplicity, simplicity, simplicity! I say, let your affairs be as two or three, and not a hundred or a thousand; instead of a million count half a dozen, and keep your accounts on your thumb-nail. In the midst of this chopping sea of civilized life, such are the clouds and storms and quicksands and thousand-and-one items to be allowed for, that a man has to live, if he would not founder and go to the bottom and not make his port at all, by dead reckoning, and he must be a great calculator indeed who succeeds. Simplify, simplify. Instead of three meals a day, if it be necessary eat but one; instead of a hundred dishes, five; and reduce other things in proportion. Our life is like a German Confederacy, made up of petty states, with its boundary forever fluctuating, so that even a German cannot tell you how it is bounded at any moment. The nation itself, with all its so-called internal improvements, which, by the way are all external and superficial, is just such an unwieldy and overgrown establishment, cluttered with furniture and tripped up by its own traps, ruined by luxury and heedless expense, by want of calculation and a worthy aim, as the million households in the land; and the only cure for it, as for them, is in a rigid economy, a stern and more than Spartan simplicity of life and elevation of purpose. It lives too fast. Men think that it is essential that the Nation have commerce, and export ice, and talk through a telegraph, and ride thirty miles an hour, without a doubt, whether they do or not; but whether we should live like baboons or like men, is a little uncertain. If we do not get out sleepers, and forge rails, and devote days and nights to the work, but go to tinkering upon our lives to improve them, who will build railroads? And if railroads are not built, how shall we get to heaven in season? But if we stay at home and mind our business, who will want railroads? We do not ride on the railroad; it rides upon us. Did you ever think what those sleepers are that underlie the railroad? Each one is a man, an Irishman, or a Yankee man. The rails are laid on them, and they are covered with sand, and the cars run smoothly over them. They are sound sleepers, I assure you. And every few years a new lot is laid down and run over; so that, if some have the pleasure of riding on a rail, others have the misfortune to be ridden upon. And when they run over a man that is walking in his sleep, a supernumerary sleeper in the wrong position, and wake him up, they suddenly stop the cars, and make a hue and cry about it, as if this were an exception. I am glad to know that it takes a gang of men for every five miles to keep the sleepers down and level in their beds as it is, for this is a sign that they may sometime get up again.

　　Why should we live with such hurry and waste of life? We are determined to be starved before we are hungry. Men say that a stitch in time saves nine, and so they take a thousand stitches today to save nine tomorrow. As for work, we haven't any of any consequence. We have the Saint Vitus' dance, and cannot possibly keep our heads still. If I should only give a few pulls at the parish bell-rope, as for a fire, that is, without setting the bell, there is hardly a man on his farm in the outskirts of Concord, notwithstanding that press of engagements which was his excuse so many times this morning, nor a boy, nor a woman, I might almost say, but would forsake all and follow that sound, not mainly to save property from the flames, but, if we will confess the truth, much more to see it burn, since burn it must, and we, be it known, did not set it on fire—or to see it put out, and have a hand in it, if that is done as handsomely; yes, even if it were the parish church itself. Hardly a man takes a half-hour's nap after dinner, but when he wakes he holds up his head and asks, "What's the news?", as if the rest of mankind had stood his sentinels. Some give directions to be waked every half-hour, doubtless for no other purpose; and then, to pay for it, they tell what they have dreamed. After a night's sleep the news is as indispensable as the breakfast. "Pray tell me anything new that has happened to a man anywhere on this globe"—and he reads it over his coffee and rolls, that a man has had his eyes gouged out this morning on the Wachito River; never dreaming the while that he lives in the dark unfathomed mammoth cave of this world, and has but the rudiment of an eye himself.

For my part, I could easily do without the post-office. I think that there are very few important communications made through it. To speak critically, I never received more than one or two letters in my life—I wrote this some years ago—that were worth the postage. The penny-post is, commonly, an institution through which you seriously offer a man that penny for his thoughts which is so often safely offered in jest. And I am sure that I never read any memorable news in a newspaper. If we read of one man robbed, or murdered, or killed by accident, or one house burned, or one vessel wrecked, or one steamboat blown up, or one cow run over on the Western Railroad, or one mad dog killed, or one lot of grasshoppers in the winter—we never need read of another. One is enough. If you are acquainted with the principle, what do you care for a myriad instances and applications? To a philosopher all news, as it is called, is gossip, and they who edit and read it are old women over their tea. Yet not a few are greedy after this gossip. There was such a rush, as I hear, the other day at one of the offices to learn the foreign news by the last arrival, that several large squares of plate glass belonging to the establishment were broken by the pressure—news which I seriously think a ready wit might write a twelve-month, or twelve years, beforehand with sufficient accuracy. As for Spain, for instance, if you know how to throw in Don Carlos and the Infanta, and Don Pedro and Seville and Granada, from time to time in the right proportions—they may have changed the names a little since I saw the papers—and serve up a bull-fight when other entertainments fail, it will be true to the letter, and give us as good an idea of the exact state or ruin of things in Spain as the most succinct and lucid reports under this head in the newspapers: and as for England, almost the last significant scrap of news from that quarter was the revolution of 1649; and if you have learned the history of her crops for an average year, you never need attend to that thing again, unless your speculations are of a merely pecuniary character. If one may judge who rarely looks into the newspapers, nothing new does ever happen in foreign parts, a French revolution not excepted.

What news! How much more important to know what that is which was never old! "Kieou-he-yu (great dignitary of the state of Wei) sent a man to Khoung-tseu to know his news. Khoung-tseu caused the messenger to be seated near him, and questioned him in these terms: What is your master doing? The messenger answered with respect: My master desires to diminish the number of his faults, but he cannot come to the end of them. The messenger being gone, the philosopher remarked: What a worthy messenger! What a worthy messenger!" The preacher, instead of vexing the ears of drowsy farmers on their day of rest at the end of the week—for

Sunday is the fit conclusion of an ill-spent week, and not the fresh and brave beginning of a new one—with this one other draggle-tail of a sermon, should shout with thundering voice, "Pause! Avast! Why so seeming fast, but deadly slow?"

Shams and delusions are esteemed for soundest truths, while reality is fabulous. If men would steadily observe realities only, and not allow themselves to be deluded, life, to compare it with such things as we know, would be like a fairy tale and the Arabian Nights' Entertainments. If we respected only what is inevitable and has a right to be, music and poetry would resound along the streets. When we are unhurried and wise, we perceive that only great and worthy things have any permanent and absolute existence, that petty fears and petty pleasures are but the shadow of the reality. This is always exhilarating and sublime. By closing the eyes and slumbering, and consenting to be deceived by shows, men establish and confirm their daily life of routine and habit everywhere, which still is built on purely illusory foundations. Children, who play life, discern its true law and relations more clearly than men, who fail to live it worthily, but who think that they are wiser by experience, that is, by failure. I have read in a Hindoo book, that "there was a king's son, who, being expelled in infancy from his native city, was brought up by a forester, and, growing up to maturity in that state, imagined himself to belong to the barbarous race with which he lived. One of his father's ministers having discovered him, revealed to him what he was, and the misconception of his character was removed, and he knew himself to be a prince. So soul", continues the Hindoo philosopher, "from the circumstances in which it is placed, mistakes its own character, until the truth is revealed to it by some holy teacher, and then it knows itself to be Brahme". I perceive that we inhabitants of New England live this mean life that we do because our vision does not penetrate the surface of things. We think that that is which appears to be. If a man should walk through this town and see only the reality, where, think you, would the "Mill-dam" go to? If he should give us an account of the realities he beheld there, we should not recognize the place in his description. Look at a meeting-house, or a court-house, or a jail, or a shop, or a dwelling-house, and say what that thing really is before a true gaze, and they would all go to pieces in your account of them. Men esteem truth remote, in the outskirts of the system, behind the farthest star, before Adam and after the last man. In eternity there is indeed something true and sublime. But all these times and places and occasions are now and here. God himself culminates in the present moment, and will never be more divine in the lapse of all the ages. And we are enabled to apprehend at all what is sublime and noble only by the perpetual instilling and drenching of the reality that surrounds us. The universe constantly and obediently answers to our conceptions; whether we travel fast or slow, the track is laid for us. Let us spend our lives in conceiving then. The poet or the artist never yet had so fair and noble a design but some of his posterity at least could accomplish it.

Let us spend one day as deliberately as Nature, and not be thrown off the track by every nutshell and mosquito's wing that falls on the rails. Let us rise early and fast, or breakfast, gently and without perturbation; let company come and let company go, let the bells ring and the children cry—determined to make a day of it. Why should we knock under and go with the stream? Let us not be upset and overwhelmed in that terrible rapid and whirlpool called a dinner, situated in the meridian shallows. Weather this danger and you are safe, for the rest of the way is down hill. With unrelaxed nerves, with morning vigor, sail by it, looking another way, tied to the mast like Ulysses. If the engine whistles, let it whistle till it is hoarse for its pains. If the bell rings, why should we run? We will consider what kind of music they are like. Let us settle ourselves, and work and wedge our feet downward through the mud and slush of opinion, and prejudice, and tradition, and delusion, and appearance, that alluvion which covers the globe, through Paris and London, through New York and Boston and Concord, through Church and State, through poetry and philosophy and religion, till we come to a hard bottom and rocks in place, which we can call reality, and say, this is, and no mistake; and then begin, having a point d'appui, below freshet and frost and fire, a place where you might found a wall or a state, or set a lamp-post safely, or perhaps a gauge, not a Nilometer, but a Realometer, that future ages might know how deep a freshet of shams and appearances had gathered from time to time. If you stand right fronting and face to face to a fact, you will see the sun glimmer on both its surfaces, as if it were a cimeter, and feel its sweet edge dividing you through the heart and marrow, and so you will happily conclude your mortal career. Be it life or death, we crave only reality. If we are really dying, let us hear the rattle in our throats and feel cold in the extremities; if we are alive, let us go about our business.

Time is but the stream I go a-fishing in. I drink at it; but while I drink I see the sandy bottom and detect how shallow it is. Its thin current slides away, but eternity remains. I would drink deeper; fish in the sky, whose bottom is pebbly with stars. I cannot count one. I know not the first letter of the alphabet. I have always been regretting that I was not as wise as the day I was born. The intellect is a cleaver; it discerns and rifts its way into the secret of things. I do not wish to be any more busy with my hands than is necessary. My head is hands and feet. I feel all my best faculties concentrated in it. My instinct tells me that my head is an organ for burrowing, as some creatures use their snout and fore paws, and with it I would mine and burrow my way through these hills. I think that the richest vein is somewhere hereabouts; so by the divining-rod and thin rising vapors I judge; and here I will begin to mine.

This Was My Mother

By Mark Twain

My mother, Jane Lampton Clemens, died in her 88th year, a mighty age for one who at 40 was so delicate of body as to be accounted a confirmed invalid destined to pass soon away. But the invalid who, forgetful of self, takes a strenuous and indestructible interest in everything and everybody, as she did, and to whom a dull moment is an unknown thing, is a formidable adversary for disease.

She had a heart so large that everybody's griefs and joys found welcome in it. One of her neighbors never got over the way she received the news of a local accident. When he had told how a man had been thrown from his horse and killed because a calf had run in his way, my mother asked with genuine interest, "What became of the calf?" She was not indifferent to the man's death; she was interested in the calf, too.

She could find something to excuse and as a rule to love in the toughest of human beings or animals—even if she had to invent it. Once we beguiled her into saying a soft word for the devil himself. We started abusing him, one conspirator after another adding his bitter word, until she walked right into the trap. She admitted that the indictment was sound, but had he been treated fairly?

She never used large words, yet when her pity or indignation was stirred she was the most eloquent person I have ever heard. We had a little slave boy whom we had hired from someone there in Hannibal. He had been taken from his family in Maryland, brought halfway across the continent, and sold. All day long he was singing, whistling, yelling, laughing. The noise was maddening, and one day I lost my temper, went raging to my mother and said Sandy had been singing for an hour straight, and I couldn't stand it. Wouldn't she please shut him up? The tears came into her eyes and she said: "Poor thing, when he sings it shows me that he is not remembering, and that comforts me; but when he is still I am afraid he is thinking. He will never see his mother again; if he can sing, I must be thankful for it. If you were older you would understand, and that friendless child's noise would make you glad."

All dumb animals had a friend in her. Hunted and disreputable cats recognized her at a glance as their refuge and champion. We once had 19 cats at one time. They were a vast burden, but they were out of luck, and that was enough. She generally had a cat in her lap when she sat down, but she denied indignantly that she liked cats better than children though there was one advantage to a cat, she'd say. You could always put it down when you were tired of holding it.

I was as much of a nuisance as any small boy and a neighbor asked her once, "Do you ever believe anything that boy says?"

"He is the wellspring of truth," my mother replied, "but you can't bring up the whole well with only one bucket. I know his average, so he never deceives me. I discount him 90 percent for embroidery and what is left is perfect and priceless truth, without a flaw."

She had a horror of snakes and bats, which I hid in pockets and sewing baskets; otherwise she was entirely fearless. One day I saw a vicious devil of a Corsican, a common terror in the town, chasing his grown daughter with a heavy rope in his hand, threatening to wear it out on her. Cautious male citizens let him pass but my mother spread her door wide to the refugee, and then, instead of closing and locking it after her, stood in it, barring the way. The man swore, cursed, threatened her with his rope; but she only stood, straight and fine, and lashed him, shamed him, derided and defied him until he asked her pardon, gave her his rope and said with a blasphemous oath that she was the bravest woman he ever saw. He and she were always good friends after that. He found in her a long-felt want—somebody who was not afraid of him.

One day in St. Louis she walked out into the street and surprised a burly cartman who was beating his horse over the head with the butt of a heavy whip. She took the whip away from him and made such a persuasive appeal that he was tripped into saying he was to blame, and into volunteering a promise that he would never abuse a horse again.

She was never too old to get up early to see the circus procession enter town. She adored parades, lectures, conventions, camp meetings, church revivals—in fact every kind of dissipation that could not be proved to have anything irreligious about it, and she never missed a funeral. She excused this preference by saying that, if she did not go to other people's funerals, they would not come to hers.

She was 82 and living in Keokuk when, unaccountably, she insisted upon attending a convention of old settlers of the Mississippi Valley. All the way there, and it was some distance, she was young again with excitement and eagerness. At the hotel she asked immediately for Dr. Barrett, of St. Louis. He had left for home that morning and would not be back, she was told. She turned away, the fire all gone from her, and asked to go home. Once there she sat silent and thinking for many days, then told us that when she was 18 she had loved a young medical student with all her heart. There was a misunderstanding and he left the country, she had immediately married, to show him that she did not care. She had never seen him since and then she had read in a newspaper that he was going to attend the old settlers' convention. "Only three hours before we reached that hotel he had been there," she mourned.

She had kept that pathetic burden in her heart 64 years without any of us suspecting it. Before the year was out, her memory began to fail. She would write letters to school-mates who had been dead 40 years, and wonder why they never answered. Four years later she died.

But to the last she was capable with her tongue. I had always been told that I was a sickly child who lived mainly on medicines during the first seven years of my life. The year she died I asked her about this and said,

"I suppose that during all that time you were uneasy about me?"

"Yes, the whole time."

"Afraid I wouldn't live?"

After a recollective pause—ostensibly to think out the facts—

"No—afraid you would."

Jane Lampton Clemens' character, striking and lovable, appears in my books as Tom Sawyer's Aunt Polly. I fitted her out with a dialect and tried to think up other improvements for her, but did not find any.

The Three New Yorks

By Elwyn Brooks White

There are roughly three New Yorks. There is, first, the New York of the man or woman who was born here, who takes the city for granted and accepts its size and its turbulence as natural and inevitable. Second, there is the New York of the commuter—the city that is devoured by locusts each day and spat out each night. Third, there is the New York of the person who was born somewhere else and came to New York in quest of something. Of these three trembling cities the greatest is the last—the city of final destination, the city that is a goal. It is this third city that accounts for New York's high-strung disposition, its poetical deportment, its dedication to the arts, and its incomparable achievements.

Commuters give the city its tidal restlessness; natives give it solidity and continuity; but the settlers give it passion. And whether it is a farmer arriving from Italy to set up a small grocery store in a slum, or a young girl arriving from a small town in Mississippi to escape the indignity of being observed by her neighbors, or a boy arriving from the Corn Belt with a manuscript in his suitcase and a pain in his heart, it makes no difference: each embraces New York with the intense excitement of first love, each absorbs New York with the fresh eyes of an adventurer, each generates heat and light to dwarf the Consolidated Edison Company.

The commuter is the queerest bird of all. The suburb he inhabits has no essential vitality of its own and is a mere roost where he comes at day's end to go to sleep. Except in rare cases, the man who lives in Mamaroneck or Little Neck or Teaneck, and works in New York, discovers nothing much about the city except the time of arrival and departure of trains and buses, and the path to a quick lunch. He is desk-bound, and has never, idly roaming in the gloaming, stumbled suddenly on Belvedere Tower in the park, seen the ramparts rise sheer from the water of the pond, and the boys along the shore fishing for minnows, girls stretched out negligently on the shelves of the rocks; he has never come suddenly on anything at all in New York as a loiterer, because he had no time between trains. He has fished in Manhattan's wallet and dug out coins, but has never listened to Manhattan's breathing, never awakened to its morning, never dropped off to sleep in its night.

About 400,000 men and women come charging onto the Island each week-day morning, out of the mouths of tubes and tunnels. Not many among them have ever spent a drowsy afternoon in the great rustling oaken silence of the reading room of the Public Library, with the book elevator (like an old water wheel) spewing out books onto the trays. They tend their furnaces in Westchester and in Jersey, but have never seen the furnaces of the Bowery, the fires that burn in oil drums on zero winter nights. They may work in the financial district downtown and never see the extravagant plantings of Rockefeller Center—the daffodils and grape hyacinths and birches of the flags trimmed to the wind on a fine morning in spring. Or they may work in a midtown office and may let a whole year swing round without sighting Governor's Island from the sea wall.

The commuter dies with tremendous mileage to his credit, but he is no rover. His entrances and exits are more devious than those in a prairie-dog village; and he calmly plays bridge while his train is buried in the mud at the bottom of the East River. The Long Island Rail Road along carried forty million commuters last year; but many of them were the same fellow retracing his steps.

The terrain of New York is such that a resident sometimes travels farther, in the end, than a commuter. The journey of the composer Irving Berlin from Cherry Street in the lower East Side to an apartment uptown was through an alley and was only three or four miles in length; but it was like going three times around the world.